T0329382

AMPHIBIOUS WARFARE

AND

COMBINED OPERATIONS

Admiral of the Fleet Sir Roger Keyes as 'Director of Combined Operations' 17th July 1940—19th October 1941

AMPHIBIOUS WARFARE
AND
COMBINED OPERATIONS

BY

ADMIRAL OF THE FLEET

THE LORD KEYES

G.C.B., K.C.V.O., C.M.G., D.S.O., D.C.L., LL.D.

LEES KNOWLES LECTURES, 1943

Second Edition
With eight maps at end

CAMBRIDGE

AT THE UNIVERSITY PRESS

1943

CAMBRIDGE
UNIVERSITY PRESS

University Printing House, Cambridge CB2 8BS, United Kingdom

Published in the United States of America by Cambridge University Press, New York

Cambridge University Press is part of the University of Cambridge.

It furthers the University's mission by disseminating knowledge in the pursuit of
education, learning and research at the highest international levels of excellence.

www.cambridge.org
Information on this title: www.cambridge.org/9781107418776

© Cambridge University Press 1943

First edition, June 1943
Second edition with maps, September 1943
First published 1943
First paperback edition 2014

A catalogue record for this publication is available from the British Library

ISBN 978-1-107-41877-6 Paperback

CONTENTS

*Maps II, III and IV by kindness of Messrs G. G. Harrap & Sons
Maps VI and VII by kindness of Messrs Thornton Butterworth*

FOREWORD

I feel it a great honour to have been invited to give the Lees Knowles lectures, which were founded to encourage the study of military science.

I have chosen 'Amphibious Warfare and Combined Operations' as my theme because it is a form of warfare which is responsible for the foundation of our great world-wide Empire, and which is vitally important, if we are to wage war across the Narrow Seas, maintain what we hold in distant oceans, and recover the Far Eastern possessions which we have lost, through our folly in trusting to other means than Sea Supremacy for our security.

To launch and maintain an amphibious operation, it is necessary to possess Sea Supremacy in the theatre of the enterprise, and with the advent of Air Power it can only be obtained by a Navy possessing the means to fight, not only on the surface and submerged, but also in the air above. When the military campaign is opened, although strategic bombing can be of great value, it is even more important that the Military Commander should have complete control over all the aircraft he needs, both to work with his ground forces and to defeat the enemy in the air.

The lessons of history are invaluable and the record of scores of amphibious operations—some brilliantly successful, others disastrous—are available from which to gain inspiration and guidance. But as a race we are slow to learn and quick to forget, and the lessons that we might have learnt from a study of previous operations are often only learnt by trial and error and bitter experience in each successive generation.

This is as true to-day as it was in 1759, when Thomas More Molyneux in *Conjunct Expeditions* reflected bitterly on our failure to profit by past experience:

'Thus shall we go again, should we stand with our arms across, despairing of ever learning better, though so strongly urged and stimulated by past errors and past misfortunes.'

'...It is a palpable demonstration, from the number of conjunct armaments these Kingdoms have fitted out, and the many fruitless attempts that have been the issue of them, that there has been no right industry, no skill or watchful observation. That is, we have never employed our minds in the study of this war 'til we have been called upon to make use of our bodies also. Thus when it is too late, by knowing nothing beforehand we doubly fatigue our mental faculties, with the vain hope of retrieving lost opportunities.'

However, in that same year, 1759, General Wolfe and Admiral Saunders brought off a 'Conjunct Expedition' in North America, which laid the foundations of the great Dominion of Canada; a campaign which is a classic and an example of Naval and Military co-operation at its best.

I therefore give a brief account of this campaign, since there is much to be learnt from it, and have followed it with my own personal experiences in three 'Combined Operations' in past wars —China 1900, Gallipoli 1915, and the Belgian Coast 1918— ending with this war as far as possible.

These lectures are now published, in the hope that they may be of some help to a younger generation.

I have to thank Messrs Harrap and Messrs Eyre & Spottiswoode for permission to quote a few passages from my earlier books.

KEYES
A. F.

TINGEWICK HOUSE,

BUCKINGHAM

MARCH 1943

CHAPTER I

COMBINED OPERATIONS IN THE
ST LAWRENCE RIVER, 1759

(*See Map I, p. 103*)

I had always been deeply interested in the capture of Quebec, and the good comradeship and the achievements of General Wolfe and Admiral Saunders and their respective commands were a shining example of Naval and Military co-operation, and we soldiers and sailors strove to live up to their traditions throughout the Gallipoli Campaign of 1915.

My knowledge of the operations in the St Lawrence River was then limited to books and maps, but in August 1934 I had the good fortune to spend some days in Quebec, and had the opportunity of studying Wolfe's two battles, under the guidance of Major Wood, whose knowledge of them and of the locality is second to none. Later I spent some time in the Archives Museum at Ottawa with another great authority—Dr Doughty.

The capture of Quebec was a vital link in the elder Pitt's scheme for the security and the extension of the British Colonies in North America, and he directed the preparations and the proceedings with extraordinary energy.

His selection of Wolfe for the Military Command was a happy one. In those days of almost constant warfare, promotion sometimes came swiftly to those who merited it.

Wolfe commanded a regiment at the age of 23, and was Quartermaster General of the Army in the abortive expedition to Rochfort at 30, and at the age of 31 he commanded a Brigade and greatly distinguished himself in the capture of Louisburg.

At Rochfort he realized the immense possibilities of Naval and Military co-operation, and commented caustically on that ill-conducted enterprise thus: '...in war something must be allowed to chance and fortune, seeing that it is in its nature hazardous and an option of difficulties; that the greatness of an object should come under consideration as opposed to the impediments that lie in the way;...The famous Council sat from morning until late at night, and the result of the debates was unanimously not to attack the place they were ordered to attack, and for reasons which no soldier will allow to be sufficient.' After the capture of Louisburg, Wolfe wrote a warm appreciation of the generous help the Army had received from Admirals Boscawen and Hardy and the seamen and marines of the Fleet.

Lord Anson, the First Lord, was responsible for the selection of Admiral Saunders, who had accompanied him during the greater part of his voyage round the world, and thus he had opportunities of appreciating his admirable qualities, which fitted him for command in a Combined Operation.

Pitt's letters to the principal officers concerned were an inspiration. The concluding passage in the secret instructions to General Wolfe is of particular interest.

Secret Instructions to General Saunders

'Whereas the Success of this Expedition will very much depend upon an entire Good Understanding between our Land and Sea Officers, We do hereby strictly enjoin and require you, on your part, to maintain and cultivate such a good Understanding and Agreement, and to order that the Soldiers under Your Command, shall man the ships when there shall be occasion for them, and when they can be spared from the Land Service, as the Commander-in-Chief of Our Squadron is instructed on His Part to entertain and cultivate the same good Understanding and Agreement and to order the Sailors and Marines, under his Command to assist our Land Forces, and to man the Batteries when there shall be occasion for them and when they can be spared from the Sea Service; and in order to establish the strictest Union that may be, between You and the Commander-in-Chief of Our Ships, You are hereby required to communicate these instructions to Him as he is required to communicate those he shall receive from Us to You.'

Admiral Saunders had under his command Rear Admirals Holmes and Durrell with twenty-two ships of the line, seventeen frigates and sloops and about 120 transports, store ships and auxiliaries.

General Wolfe's army consisted of three Brigades under Brigadier Generals Murray, Townshend and Monkton (between 9000 and 10,000 men).

The French having removed all the buoys, and having destroyed all the aids to navigation in the St Lawrence, had good reason to hope that a fleet of vessels sufficient to carry an expeditionary force large enough to capture Quebec would not succeed in overcoming the intricate navigation of a difficult passage, known as the Traverse, some miles below Quebec.

It happened that James Cook, who afterwards became famous as a great navigator, was Master of one of Admiral Durrell's ships, which preceded the main force, and his log describes how the passage was 'sounded out' and how he 'acquainted' himself with 'ye channel'.

To the consternation of the French on 26th–27th June, 1759, Saunders with 141 sail anchored abreast of the Isle of Orleans.

Drake's maxim—'Time...is half a victory, which being lost is irrecoverable'—was observed, and without any loss of time, Wolfe's army was landed and by the evening of the 27th was disembarked on the island without the loss of a ship or man. A violent gale sprang up after the troops were landed, which caused some damage to transport and the loss of anchors and small boats; and on the night of 28th June, seven fire-ships were sent from Quebec into the crowded anchorage. However, these were towed clear and ran aground and no damage was suffered.

The next night General Monkton's Brigade crossed the river and took up a position at Point Levi and with great energy and speed batteries of guns and mortars were mounted, to bombard Quebec across the river.

On 9th July, with two Brigades, Wolfe occupied a position on the north shore, below the falls of Montmorency, leaving a small force at the north-west point of Orleans Island.

In the meantime, Admiral Saunders had stationed his vessels in the basin and between Point Levi and Point of Orleans. On 17th July he sent some ships above the town of Quebec with a few troops on board, to give General Wolfe the opportunity of reconnoitring the river.

On 28th July the enemy made yet another determined attack with fire-stages and rafts, but had no better success than before.

On 31st July General Wolfe launched an attack in daylight against the enemy's main force, which was strongly entrenched at Beauport and along the foreshore between Montmorency River and Quebec.

The water was too shallow to allow the ships to give close support, but the *Centurion*—a 50-gun ship—was anchored between the Island of Orleans and the Montmorency River, in a position to engage the enemy's redoubts from their eastern flank, and which commanded the ford across which Townshend's and Murray's Brigades were to march, when the tide was sufficiently low.

Meanwhile, two light draft transports, which had been heavily armed for the purpose, were run ashore at high water to engage the redoubts and batteries covering the beach, on which the troops from Monkton's Brigade at Point Levi were to be landed in boats from the Fleet.

The rise and fall of tide, as in all amphibious operations, played a decisive part, and by the time it was possible for the troops to march across the ford, the tide was sufficiently low to make the landing on the muddy beach difficult. The impetuosity of the leading sea-borne troops involved them in difficulties before the main force were able to land and those advancing from the eastward were in a position to attack. Eventually, after suffering considerable loss, Wolfe decided to withdraw his troops, which he succeeded in doing before nightfall—the two transports being abandoned and burnt, as they were fast aground.

Wolfe, as was his wont, directed the proceedings personally, with utter disregard for his safety, and whilst on board one of the grounded transports, reconnoitring the position and movements of the enemy, he was hit three times by splinters and had his stick knocked out of his hand by a cannon ball.

On 5th August Saunders sent Admiral Holmes to join the ships above Quebec, and embarked about 1200 troops under Brigadier General Murray, to operate against the enemy there. They returned three weeks later, having inflicted some damage to the enemy's ammunition and store dumps, and caused a diversion.

During the later days of August, Wolfe was very ill with fever, and it is clear from the last letter that he wrote to Pitt, dated 3rd September, that he was very harassed by the difficulties of the situation, for he had come to the conclusion that even if he succeeded in beating the enemy by a frontal attack on his main position, the assault of the town would be a very hazardous proceeding, since it was covered by entrenchments and batteries, which could not be commanded by the guns of the Fleet.

Wolfe decided, therefore, to advance from above Quebec with the object of drawing the enemy from their entrenched positions below the town and bringing them to action.

I do not propose to dwell on the details of the operations which followed, but rather on the lessons to be learned from them.

It is said that General the Marquis of Montcalm—the Commander-in-Chief of the French land forces, and M. de Vaudreuil —the Governor General of the Province (a Captain in the French Navy)—were not on good terms. The General had been anxious to station 4000 troops and a considerable force of artillery, strongly entrenched at Point Levi, but the disposition—which would have been exceedingly inconvenient to Wolfe, and might well have defeated the British plan which was eventually carried out—was overruled at a Council of War by M. de Vaudreuil, who insisted that their duty was to act on the defensive with the whole of the available force on the north side of the basin, protecting every possible landing place. On no account should their forces be divided. Montcalm, apparently against his better judgment, conformed to this plan.

When the British actually seized the position Montcalm had wished to occupy, he embarked a force of 1600 men to drive them out; but to quote Wolfe—'Unluckily they fell into confusion, fired upon one another and went back again; by which we lost an opportunity of defeating this large detachment.'

Standing at the various points of vantage in Quebec—from which the French Commander-in-Chief watched the proceedings of his enemies—I could picture the whole scene, and having seen some modern battles, what struck one most was the diminutive size of the stage on which the great events were enacted, and the small number of the forces engaged.

At one time Montcalm seems to have been fairly confident that the natural strength of the position would enable him to hold out, until the winter forced his adversaries to raise the siege. The defeat of Wolfe's attack on the Beauport coast must have encouraged this view, as some weeks passed before any other considerable effort was made.

In the light of our knowledge of the strength of the French position I cannot help feeling that perhaps Wolfe was fortunate to have been repulsed at Beauport, before he was too deeply committed.

In the days that followed, the value of the command of the sea, and the wonderful mobility it gave to the Army, became more and more apparent, and we know now that the constant threat of the water-borne troops, covered by Admiral Holmes's squadron above Quebec, caused the deepest anxiety to Montcalm and ceaseless vigil to General Bougainville—who commanded the French troops on the western flank.

When Wolfe decided not to repeat his attack on the Beauport position, the transfer of the British troops and batteries from the Montmorency Falls was skilfully effected without the loss of a single man on 3rd September. Troops and batteries were then concentrated on the south side of the St Lawrence opposite

Quebec. A small force was left on the island of Orleans with orders to make themselves as conspicuous as possible.

Three thousand men were embarked in the transports and kept afloat above Quebec ready to land anywhere, and water transport was standing by to take the remainder wherever they might be required. Thus the French were kept on the *qui vive* for a distance of 30 miles, and General Bougainville's force wearily marched and counter-marched for three weeks, trying to keep pace with the various threatened landings.

On 12th September all was ready to carry out Wolfe's plan. The vessels above Quebec were constantly under way, and manœuvred to convey the impression that a landing would take place at a point 13 miles above Quebec. Saunders made a very successful feint, by putting all his Marines in boats and standing in towards ·Beauport just before dark. During the night he laid buoys inshore, to make the French think that the ships would move in at daylight to cover a landing there.

The main attack was to be made by Monkton's and Murray's Brigades at Foulon, the one accessible approach to the Heights of Abraham, Wolfe being with Admiral Holmes in the flagship of the squadron covering the transports. Meanwhile the batteries on the south shore were heavily bombarding Quebec all night.

At 4 a.m. on 13th September the attack was launched, Wolfe and his Staff in the leading boat being the first to spring ashore. The landing was carried out so quietly that the small French post at Foulon was surprised, and the battery 300 yards to the west was taken in reverse and captured. By 8 a.m. Wolfe had nearly 5000 men in battle order across the Plains of Abraham, awaiting Montcalm's attack, while the sailors were disembarking guns and siege material.

Wolfe, who had been a sick man for some weeks and whose anxieties must have been intense, was ablaze with confident ardour during the battle, striding up and down the line encouraging his troops. He was twice hit before he received his mortal wound,

but lived long enough to know that the French were in full retreat and that victory was assured.

The forcing of the St Lawrence and the capture of Quebec were
the first steps to the winning of the great Canadian Dominion,
which now stretches from the Atlantic to the Pacific; but it is well
to remember that we should have lost Quebec the following
spring, but for our command of the sea and the timely arrival of
a British Squadron some weeks before the passage of the river was
considered possible. In the meantime, weakened by scurvy and
fever, our small garrison, under General Murray, were themselves besieged in Quebec by a vastly superior force of French
troops under General Levis, after suffering a severe reverse within
a mile of Wolfe's victorious battle.

One can well imagine the excitement and relief of the sorely
pressed garrison, when they were able to distinguish the British
ensign flying from the approaching ships. Those ships would in
all probability have been French, but for Hawke's victory over
the French Fleet in Quiberon Bay, 3000 miles away, which gave
us the command of the sea.

As a sailor, I welcome this opportunity of paying a tribute to
the memory of Wolfe, a soldier who was such a masterly ex-
ponent of amphibious warfare, and one who appreciated to the
full the value of Sea Power.

I am sure if Wolfe had lived he would have generously
acknowledged that but for the skilful and enterprising navigation
of the Fleet up the St Lawrence River, and the devoted co-operation of Admiral Saunders and all who sailed with him, he would
never have carried out his brilliant achievement. But Wolfe's
passing in the hour of victory, like that of Nelson—whom he so
closely resembled in many characteristics—overshadowed everything, and the magnitude of the Navy's share in the victory—like
the value of Sea Power—is often forgotten.

The lessons which, I submit, stand out in the operations which
resulted in the capture of Quebec, are:

The danger of static or passive defence against an enterprising and aggressive foe. When Montcalm neglected to hold strategic points which commanded the waters adjacent to Quebec, and allowed the British to seize them, Saunders was able to cut him off from water-borne supplies and threaten, by amphibious strokes, his land communications for a distance of about 30 miles.

The power of defence over attack, even in those days, was such as to stress the importance of surprise, to effect which, highly disciplined troops trained in *night fighting* are essential to success.

CHAPTER II

THE CHINA WAR, 1900

(See Maps II, III and IV, pp. 104, 105, 106)

Early in June 1900, owing to the Boxer rising in China, about thirty men-of-war belonging to almost every nation possessing a navy assembled off Taku. Owing to shoal water, battleships and cruisers had to anchor about 4 or 5 miles from the bar across the Peiho River, which was 7 miles from the entrance, and on which there was only about 2 feet of water at low spring tides.

Vessels drawing up to 12 feet could cross the bar for two or three hours each tide and lie at anchor between Taku and Tongku, which was about 4 miles up the river. Tongku was the terminus of the only railway to Tientsin and Peking.

In 1858 a British Squadron of gunboats under Admiral Sir Michael Seymour had entered the Peiho River without opposition. In 1859 another British Squadron of gunboats, not expecting serious opposition, had tried to force a passage past the forts, and had been repulsed with heavy losses. In 1860 a combined operation was undertaken and a considerable army from India was landed at Pei-Tung, 8 miles to the north-east of the entrance to the river. The forts were captured from the rear with very slight loss, as the guns of the forts could not train inland. This secured a base for the Navy, through which the expedition to Peking was supplied.

In 1900 the entrance of the river was fortified on both sides by batteries, mounting about seventy modern Krupp and Armstrong guns of from 5 to 8 in. calibre of the most up-to-date type, whilst the garrison had been trained by Europeans. All the guns which could bear on the upper reaches of the river were on central pivot mountings and could command all the approaches from inland. From seaward the forts were really impregnable, as they were out of range of the heavy ships and only small vessels of shallow draft could enter the river, and in places they would have to go in single line ahead, owing to the narrowness of the channel; while at the entrance they would have to pass the North and South Forts at a range of about 200 yards. Pei-Tung was now also well fortified.

The British Fleet was under the command of Admiral Sir Edward Seymour, who being the senior officer present, presided over the conferences of the Allied Admirals.

On 9th June information was received from Peking that all the European Ministers were taking shelter in the British Legation, it being the best adapted for defence, but that unless help was received soon, it would be too late. It was decided to land naval detachments at once, and Sir Edward Seymour undertook to lead an International Force to the relief of the Legations.

British seamen and marines were taken up the river that night in destroyers, tugs and lighters, past the forts, which although alert and evidently excited, did not open fire. The Naval Brigade were landed at Tongku, where they entrained for Tientsin. I took the Admiral and about 200 men up in the destroyer *Fame* and, when he landed, he told me to offer to bring in any of the foreigners who had not yet sent their men in.

I could not cross the bar until daylight, and the guns of the forts trained on the *Fame* and followed her out, but again did not fire. Finding that all our people and everyone except the Russians had been landed, I ran alongside the Russian flagship and offered to take her Naval Brigade up to Tongku. After a considerable delay, 240 seamen were produced, a very small contribution from the numerous Russian ships. I took them in on the same tide, but they arrived at Tientsin too late to join the International Relief Force— 2000 strong, about half of them British—which had already left by train for Peking; this, I think, was the Russian Admiral's intention. Altogether about 300 British and 300 foreign seamen remained at Tientsin and were joined by 1700 Russian soldiers with some guns for the defence of the foreign settlement there.

The next day Admiral Bruce—second in command of the

Station—arrived in the *Barfleur* and I took 150 of her men—under the command of Commander David Beatty—up to Tongku, where they entrained for Tientsin.

On 14th June we learnt that the Allied Relief Force had been cut off, the railway between Tientsin and Peking having been cut behind it, and that Chinese Imperial troops were closing in on Tientsin. That evening telephone and telegraphic communication with Tientsin was cut.

On 15th June the *Fame* was lying off Taku waiting for the tide, in order to return to the Fleet, when I received a message from Admiral Bruce directing me to go to Tientsin at once, but to return in time to come out on the evening tide and report on the situation.

On arriving at Tongku, I found that the (English) station-master had just received orders to send all the rolling stock to Lutai, where there was a large concentration of Chinese Imperial troops, to take them to Tientsin and Tongku. The Captain of a German sloop, which was lying alongside the wharf, told me he would not let them go, and would have them shunted into a siding under his guns.

Tongku is about 27 miles from Tientsin. On arriving there I found a train of carriages and trucks standing in Tientsin Station, crowded with Chinese troops, who shouted insults at me.

I reported to Captain Bayly of H.M.S. *Aurora*, the senior officer, who told me that Admiral Seymour had not been heard of since 13th June, when a letter was received from him ordering a detachment to be sent to Lofa (40 miles from Tientsin) to establish a base and supply depot there. Three attempts had been made to reach Lofa, but the railway was hopelessly broken and the detachment had to return to Tientsin.

Captain Bayly said he could not get in touch with Admiral Seymour, who had started on what he thought would be a four-hour journey, with only two days' provisions and very little spare ammunition.

While I was talking to him, the stationmaster at Tientsin reported that he had just received a telegram from the station-master at Lutai, saying that, as no rolling stock had arrived from Tongku, a large force of Chinese troops was marching in three columns, one to Tientsin, one to Taku, and the third to the railway junction between the two.

Captain Bayly considered the situation desperate, the Imperial troops were undoubtedly going to join with the Boxers, a possibility which Admiral Seymour had evidently not anticipated, and it could only be a question of hours before Tientsin itself was cut off.

He asked me to tell Admiral Bruce that reinforcements, provisions and ammunition were urgently needed, that immediate action was necessary, and he considered it imperative to capture the Taku Forts and occupy Taku and Tongku.

A few minutes later, another message came from the station-master, saying that the troops I had seen entrained had been ordered to Tongku to reinforce the garrison of the Taku Forts.

It was obviously important that Admiral Bruce, who was completely out of touch, should be informed at once, and we rick-shawed to the station, in the hope of my being able to get a lift in the troop train, but it had just left—rather to my relief! After some delay a Chinese driver and fireman were found who—for a considerable reward—undertook to take me to Tongku on an engine. As we approached the junction, which had been deserted when I passed through it on my way up, we saw it was crowded with Chinese troops, and as the engine-driver was inclined to slow up, I had to encourage him to increase speed with my revolver, and we rocketed through, much relieved that we were not diverted into a siding.

On arriving at Tongku, I told the German Captain that I was going out to the Fleet, to urge the taking of the Taku Forts at once. He was in full agreement and gave me a letter to take out to his Admiral.

Fortunately there were a number of gunboats in the river. The British sloop *Algerine*—commanded by a very stout-hearted officer, Commander Johnston Stewart—was lying off the Taku Forts with the *Fame*; three Russian gunboats were in the reach above; a Japanese gunboat, which was under repair with her engines out of action, was alongside a wharf below Tongku; and a German, a French and a very old United States paddle gunboat were lying alongside the wharf at Tongku. Between them and the Russians, four modern very fast German-built Chinese destroyers were lying alongside the Naval Arsenal, between Taku and Tongku.

I did not dare take the *Fame* out, as I had been ordered, as I feared that, once outside, I might never be allowed in again, so commandeered a large shallow draft tug to take me out to the Fleet.

Captain Johnston Stewart told me to tell the Admiral that he fully agreed that the Taku Forts should be captured. The guns of the forts followed the tug out as usual.

I arrived alongside the *Barfleur* during the night. When Admiral Bruce heard what I had to say, he gave orders for the tug to be filled with ammunition and provisions for Tientsin, and told me that he would ask the Russian Admiral—who was now senior officer afloat—to summon a conference in the morning.

I begged him to allow the *Whiting*—our other destroyer—to join me in the river, to ensure the capture of the Chinese destroyers, before they could do any damage, and he agreed.

I started back on the same tide and looked down the muzzles of the guns of the forts as we entered the river at dawn.

The *Algerine*, which lay right under the guns of the North-West Fort, reported that the forts were at action stations all night!

The contents of the tug were sent to Tientsin by rail, with a small guard, who returned that evening. We heard nothing more from Tientsin for several days.

Two tugs were sent out to the *Barfleur*, one returned laden with stores and ammunition for Tientsin, the other brought in 320 officers and men, under Commander Craddock (who later lost his life at the Battle of Coronel). These were the gleanings of the

British Fleet, a few lieutenants and midshipmen who had been left behind, quartermasters, boatswains, armourers, blacksmiths, coopers, carpenters, stokers, boys and bandsmen, who had volunteered. They were armed with the few remaining rifles, cutlasses, pistols, tomahawks and boarding pikes, and Commander Craddock's ardent spirit seemed to have entered into his strange little army.

This was the British contribution to the assaulting force for the attack on the Taku Forts. The French were not represented. The Italians sent 25 seamen under an officer, who asked to be allowed to join the British force, and they were embarked in the *Algerine* with our men. About 250 Japanese sailors came in and joined their gunboat. The Germans sent 3 officers and 133 seamen, and the Austrians 2 officers and 20 men, who all went to the German gunboat. The Russians only provided 159 soldiers, who were encamped at Tongku, although they might have sent hundreds of seamen as their whole Asiatic Squadron was anchored off Taku, fully manned, the few men they had already landed having been replaced by men from their base at Port Arthur. The Russian Admiral evidently had orders to keep his fleet intact.

Russia had succeeded in getting so much out of the existing Chinese Government, that it was all to her interest—for the moment at any rate—to sit on the fence and let the other nations fall foul of China. We were told later that the Russian Admiral had got into great trouble with his Government for having agreed to the taking of the forts.

Admiral Bruce wrote to Commander Johnston Stewart that the foreign Admirals and Senior Naval Officers had decided that as the Chinese Imperial troops were acting aggressively, it was necessary to secure a base in the Peiho River, in order to maintain communications with the forces up country. If the vessels in the river were destroyed, as they might be at any moment if the Chinese fired on them, the whole force up country would be cut off. The conference recognized that the forts were impregnable from seaward and decided to deliver an ultimatum to the General

Commanding, that in view of the menacing attitude of the forts and the fact that Chinamen had been observed laying mines, the Allied Powers intended to occupy the forts at 2 a.m. on 17th June. If no resistance was offered, they would be handed back intact, when matters had been settled.

Admiral Bruce directed Commander Johnston Stewart to act in conjunction with the Allied Forces, under the command of the senior Russian Captain. He went on to say that the American Admiral declined to take part in the attack, as he had had no instructions from his Bureau. So it was decided that the United States gunboat was to stay above Tongku and embark all the families of the foreign community and fugitive missionaries from various inland stations, who had fled from the murderous Boxer rising.

The Russian Captain summoned the senior officers of the Allied ships and Commander Craddock on board his ship to a Council of War. Commander Johnston Stewart assured the Council that the *Fame* and *Whiting* would guarantee the capture of the four Chinese destroyers, in time to prevent them torpedoing any vessels in the river or outside. The Council decided that they would not commence the attack until 4 a.m., just before daylight, and that after dark, the *Algerine*, *Fame* and *Whiting* should move into a less exposed position.

At 2 a.m. the *Fame* and *Whiting*, under my command, were to attack the four destroyers, to clear the passage by 3 a.m. for the German and French gunboats to join the other vessels. The Assaulting Force was to be landed at 2.30 a.m. and to line a long ditch about 1000 yards from the North-West Fort and assault the fort when it was sufficiently reduced by the gunfire of the ships.

It was very important that our destroyers should do their business as quietly as possible, so as not to disturb the forts, and while the tide was still ebbing, so I arranged that the *Fame* should get under way at 1.30 a.m., followed by the *Whiting* at a distance of about 300 yards (the distance between the first and third

Chinese destroyers); each vessel was to have a boarding party of eight men, armed with cutlasses and pistols on her forecastle, and tow a whaler—commanded by her First Lieutenant with a boarding party of twelve men similarly armed. The boarding parties were to be covered by six men with rifles, the guns were to be manned but were not to be fired unless absolutely necessary. This employed all our seamen and exhausted all our arms. In the *Fame* the stokers who could be spared from the stokehold and engine-room were armed with iron bars and pokers, to prevent the Chinese—who greatly outnumbered our small boarding parties—from boarding us.

At 9 p.m. it was pitch dark and the *Algerine*, *Whiting* and *Fame* got under way very quietly and anchored just below the nearest Russians.

The ultimatum was delivered at 10 p.m. and the Chinese General replied that he would be glad to hand over the forts, but he would have to obey orders, which was understood to mean that he would have to consult a higher authority. No one seemed to have anticipated that the Chinese would take the initiative, which they did at 12.50 a.m. A single gun was fired from the South Fort, followed by what appeared to be a simultaneous discharge of every gun in all the forts. It was very fortunate that we had moved our anchorage, as they did not succeed in hitting the *Algerine* until daylight, but the three Russian gunboats had occupied the same position for some days and probably every gun in the South Fort which could bear had been laid on them before dark. One was sunk; but fortunately she only had 2 feet of water under her, and another was seriously damaged.

The *Fame* and *Whiting* got under way immediately and stood up the centre of the river, as if we were going to Tongku, but when we were abreast of the Chinese destroyers, we sheered in and boarded all four simultaneously, taking them completely by surprise, and driving their crews overboard or below, capturing them all without losing a man. However, as we were in a very exposed position, with guns firing at us, and being sniped from the Dockyard, I landed a party to clear the Dockyard, and then we towed our prizes up to Tongku.

Meanwhile, having made a signal to the gunboats reporting that the passage was clear, the German and French gunboats came down and took station above the *Algerine*.

This all took some time and we were directly in line with the South Fort and the *Algerine* and German gunboat, so came in for everything that passed over them. The *Whiting* was hit, and later a fire started on board her and she ran ashore, and it took some time to tow her off; this all delayed our going down the river to join in the fight against the forts.

On our way down about 6 a.m., I found the tug, which was loaded with ammunition and stores for Tientsin, sheltering in the bend of the river. I directed her to go up to Tientsin at once, as her cargo was urgently required there, but the Midshipman in charge reported that the Chinese crew refused to take her past a fort called Hsi-Cheng, about 12 miles up the river. I did not know of the existence of this fort, or its strength, and having no intelligence books on board, I ran alongside the Japanese gunboat and asked the commanding officer if he could tell me anything about it. He produced a book, in which it was described as being situated 400 yards from the river on the south side, armed with 43 guns, mostly obsolete, but with some modern 6 in. guns. I knew nothing about the pilotage of the river above Tongku, but the tug had a pilot on board, so I told the Midshipman to go up the river full speed, and the *Fame* and *Whiting* would follow in her wake.

We stopped abreast of the fort, until the tug was well out of range above it; we could see six 6 in. guns on the parapet, which was crowded with men; however, they did not fire, and as we could do nothing against such a formidable obstacle, we returned to Taku, and found that all three forts were in our hands.

While we had been engaged in the upper reaches of the river, the action had raged below us from 12.50 a.m. until 7 a.m. At one time the situation looked very serious, as the assaulting force, which had landed on the north shore, directly the Chinese had opened fire, were held up by the fire of the North-West Fort, on which the fire of the ships seemed to make very little impression. Eventually the *Algerine*, followed by the German gunboat, got under way and laid themselves right alongside the North-West Fort and silenced it.

The British and Japanese then assaulted it with great dash, led by Commander Craddock and a Japanese Commander, who was killed upon the parapet. The British and Japanese flags went up simultaneously. Leaving the Japanese there, the British raced on to the North Fort, followed by the Germans, and our flag was the first hoisted there. Some of the guns of the North Fort were then turned on the South Fort, which had been well hammered by the three Russian gunboats for some hours.

As it appeared to be silenced, Craddock then crossed the river in boats, sent by the *Algerine*, and took possession of it. The honours of the day certainly rested with him, Commander Johnston Stewart and the Commander of the German gunboat, who was very severely wounded when his ship closed in to the North-West Fort.

Our losses were surprisingly light, amounting to only 35 killed and 137 wounded, and with the exception of the Russian ship sunk, which was eventually refloated, the damage to ships was not serious.

The Naval Base for further operations was thus secured by a Combined Operation; but there was another combined naval and military operation which, I felt very strongly, should have been carried out without any delay, namely, the capture of the Hsi-Cheng Fort, which did not seem to me to be an unsurmountable problem. It is true that the *Whiting* and the damaged German and Russian vessels had left for repairs; however, more Russian and German gunboats and Japanese destroyers had arrived, also Russian and Japanese troops, and a British battalion from Hong Kong. United States troops were also on their way from the Philippines, French from Indo-China and Indian troops from

India, who would need a base at Tientsin for their advance on Peking.

In the meantime heavy firing could be heard from the direction of Tientsin. As the railway had been torn up and its bridges destroyed, and there was no transport or Chinese labour to be obtained, Tientsin was now completely cut off from supplies, the normal route by river transport being held up by the Hsi-Cheng Fort. It looked so formidable on paper, that no one could be induced to attack it. Craddock and I made a plan to capture it by a surprise attack, and he actually collected sufficient boats to carry his Naval Brigade in tow of the *Fame*, which was to cover the landing. I went out to the *Barfleur* to ask the Admiral's permission to do this. That was an unfortunate mistake, as of course he would not hear of it. We ought to have done it without asking, and as things turned out, it would have succeeded.

I then tried to persuade the Russian Admiral and General to capture it by a combined operation. They had come down to my ship, which was lying alongside at Tongku; they said it was much too dangerous, as there was a camp of 5000 Tartar cavalry within 5 miles of it, and gunboats would be taken in detail by the guns of the fort, as they came round the bend of the river in single file. I heard later that the Russians and Germans held a council of war, to which they did not invite Commander Johnston Stewart, and decided that it was not a practicable proposition, although they had seven gunboats and at least 4000 troops available.

Meantime Sir Edward Seymour's force had disappeared into the blue; heavy firing in the neighbourhood of Tientsin was persistent, and though some reinforcements had got through, including Craddock's Naval Brigade and a British regiment, and the railway had been repaired up to within 12 miles of Tientsin, it was held up there by a bridge which could not be repaired, and the stores and ammunition so urgently needed were accumulating at this railhead. Once the river was opened, all the difficulties of supply and reinforcement would be solved. I could not get anyone to take my view seriously, or realize that it was worth any risk.

Eventually, after persistent efforts, I was given permission to 'reconnoitre' the river, provided that the *Fame* ran no risk of being fired on by the fort. However, in case of accidents, I borrowed an officer and twelve men with rifles from the *Algerine*, and all the guncotton and Bickford fuse she possessed, and arrived abreast of the fort at dawn on 27th June. As the bank was 'steep to', the *Fame* was able to lie almost alongside it. Leaving the *Fame's* guns trained on the approaches, I landed at once with thirty-two men and we ran to the gate, meaning to blow it down, but found we could get in without. There were a great many Chinamen in the fort, but they made themselves scarce. Having posted sentries to give warning of any approach from the Tartar camp, we hastily blew up the guns and laid a train to the magazine, which blew up with a terrifying explosion. The blast actually shook the Admiral's stern walk doors open, 25 miles away, and they saw a column of smoke going several hundred feet into the air—they wondered if I was on the top of it! At Taku they thought at first it was an earthquake.

I had placed my men in a well-protected casemate about 200 yards away, while I lit the fuse and then ran to join them. The blast knocked me down just as I got there, but I was able to crawl in before a mass of masonry fell from the sky. I never dreamt that anything so terrifying might happen, when I light-heartedly lit the fuse. We learnt later that the magazine contained all the ammunition of a modern siege train, as well as supplies for the fortress guns.

Our only casualties were two or three of the sentries wounded. We returned to the *Fame* as quickly as possible, and they were much relieved to see us, as they said the river bank seemed to lift and they did not think anything could have been left alive in the fort.

The river was now open and supplies and reinforcements were rushed up to Tientsin. Sir Edward Seymour's force was relieved the next day and brought back into Tientsin, but the Chinese troops investing the Foreign Settlements were not defeated until

13th July; and the Legations in Peking were not relieved until 13th August, despite the arrival at Tientsin of an Allied Army of 19,300 men and 96 guns, composed as follows:

Japanese	8500 men,	50 guns
Russians	4500 ,,	16 ,,
British	3000 ,,	12 ,,
Americans	2500 ,,	6 ,,
French	800 ,,	12 ,,

I remarked in a letter early in July: 'There are more Allied troops in the neighbourhood of Tientsin than there were British troops in the whole of India at the time of the Mutiny; and yet they have allowed themselves to be practically shut up by a few thousand Chinamen, and prevented from marching 80 miles to the relief of the Legations in Peking, which are in great peril.'

The army from India under General Sir Alfred Gaselee arrived on 26th July, and the General—who had served under my father —asked that I might be appointed as his Naval Staff Officer. I joined him at Tientsin on 28th July.

Combined Operations, whether they be carried out by the Services of one country or the Forces of Allied nations, are exceedingly difficult to put across the enemy. There are so many conflicting considerations and sometimes jealousies.

I have already mentioned the Russian outlook, to which was added the hatred and distrust of the Japanese. The Japanese for their part were looking sideways at the Russians, bitterly hating them for—with German support—having turned them out of Port Arthur which they had captured from the Chinese in 1895. At the same time the Japanese were on their best behaviour, obviously anxious to impress the Europeans with their military efficiency, contempt of death and correct conduct.

No one seemed particularly interested in relieving the Legations at Peking, except the British and Americans, and they had not sufficient force—or thought they had not—to act alone. And so time passed.

Eventually Sir Alfred Gaselee, with the support of the American General, told an Allied conference, which was presided over by the Russian General, that the British and Americans would go on without the Russians and Japanese if they delayed any longer. That stirred up things and we actually started the advance from Tientsin at dawn on 5th August.

There was some considerable opposition at Pei-Tsung, which was overcome by the Japanese, and I watched their gallant attack with admiration. The next action was at Yang-Tsun, and most of the fighting fell to the British and Americans.

There was a great deal of rivalry on the march; it was very hot and the dust was suffocating. There was only one route and no one wanted to go last, so of course the British did on every occasion.

The whole force arrived at Tung-Chau, and there we left the river, which up till then had been our main means of communication.

A council of war was held, at which the Russian General declared that his troops were too tired to advance until the following day and it was agreed that the whole force would advance on Peking the next morning. However, after nightfall, the Russians went forward as quietly as possible. The Japanese, who expected their rival's action, tried to forestall them and moved parallel with them. The Americans, getting wind of the advance, followed a little later. The first we knew of this advance was heavy gunfire in the direction of Peking and we started our march 17 miles behind our Allies.

Fortunately, our Minister in Peking had managed to get a message through to Sir Alfred to advise him to come through the Chinese city and approach the Legations through the main drain in the Tartar city wall. When the General suggested at the Allied conference that the British force would attack through the Chinese city gate, the Russians and Japanese, we heard, were much amused; the Russians had their eye on the Treasury, the Japanese also on the Treasury and the rich grain stores in the

Tartar city, and their attack was directed against the Tartar city gates, which were strongly defended.

When we arrived at the Chinese city gate late that afternoon we encountered no opposition, though on the city wall there was a large encampment, but its defenders had moved to reinforce the Chinese troops which had completely held up the Japanese and Russian assault.

At 5 p.m. the whole British force entered the Legations either through the main drain or the Tsien-Men Gate, which was captured by the advance forces which had penetrated through the drain.

A couple of hours later the Americans, who were on the left of the Russians, followed our route.

The presence of the British force in the rear of the Chinese troops, which had held up the Russian and Japanese advance all day, broke down the defence and our faithful Allies entered the Tartar city during the night.

The China campaign was full of lessons for me and had a considerable influence on my future.

Combined Operations depend for their success on a leader, who can command the single-minded loyalty of all under him, and when the force is composed of Allied Forces, with conflicting aims and jealousies, it is a pretty difficult proceeding.

The Military Force which assembled at Tientsin to relieve Peking had no leader to give it unity of command, and in consequence the Legations and foreign communities might well have perished long before relief arrived.

As I have said, I thought Peking might have been relieved two or three weeks before the British force actually arrived. Tormenting delays and inaction ensued, until the British General forced matters.

Admiral Seymour was much criticized and condemned in Tientsin, particularly by Russian soldiers, for undertaking his ill-fated expedition, which his critics described as folly, foredoomed to failure. If the cry for immediate help from the foreign

Ministers at Peking had been ignored and the worst had happened, it would have been an everlasting disgrace to us sailors. Seamen were the only people available to respond to it, and I think that we can feel proud that a British Admiral had the pluck and moral courage to make such a gallant effort, and had the personality to carry the seamen of all the other nations loyally with him when his force was cut off and suffered the loss of 65 killed and 230 wounded before it was relieved.

The outlook of the leaders of the forces of the two greatest Military Powers in Europe—Germany and Russia—was interesting. They seemed unable to appreciate that the command of the water-way, which could be used to insure their communications, was of vital importance, since land communications were poor and very difficult to maintain.

One other lesson. One so often hears it said that it is folly for ships to engage forts because their guns cannot expect to knock out the individual guns of a fort, whereas the ship presents a vulnerable target; but one cannot make arbitrary rules in war and allow them to stifle action and enterprise.

At Taku, the *Algerine* and her German consort did not succeed in knocking out a single gun until they laid themselves alongside the fort; then the heavy and accurate fire from every arm they possessed caused many casualties to the guns' crews, silenced the guns and enabled the assaulting force, which had been held up for some hours, to storm and capture the fort.

It will be seen that similar tactics were pursued when the Allied British and French Fleet attacked the outer forts of the Dardanelles fifteen years later.

CHAPTER III

THE DARDANELLES CAMPAIGN

(See Maps V and VI, pp. 107, 108)

Before embarking on the Dardanelles Campaign of 1915, I propose to tell you briefly of a previous enterprise, since we are often told that Admiral Duckworth's failure to effect anything in 1807 should have warned us of the folly of entering the Dardanelles with ships alone, and the hazard of withdrawing, if our mission failed.

In the autumn of 1806 Turkey had closed the Bosphorus and Dardanelles to the ships of our ally, Russia.

On 21st November Rear-Admiral Sir Thomas Louis, flying his flag in the *Canopus*, anchored off Tenedos with a small squadron, with orders to reconnoitre the forts and fortifications on his way to Constantinople.

On 27th November, the wind being favourable, Admiral Louis entered the Straits. After leaving two of his ships and a frigate in Sari Siglar Bay he exchanged salutes with the Castle at the Narrows, and taking careful note of the fortifications as he passed, sailed on in the *Canopus* to Constantinople.

Next day the *Canopus* anchored off Seraglio Point and remained there for a month, in company with the frigate *Endymion*, which had brought out our Ambassador—Mr Arbuthnot.

On 28th December Louis embarked the Russian Ambassador —who had broken off relations with Turkey—and rejoined his squadron in Sari Siglar Bay.

Our Ambassador and the British residents at Constantinople, fearing that they would be captured and held as hostages, in case a British force should commence hostilities, embarked in the *Endymion* and joined Admiral Louis' squadron, which withdrew to Tenedos.

Meanwhile the Admiralty had ordered Lord Collingwood to detach a force to the Dardanelles, under Vice-Admiral Sir John

Duckworth, to be ready in case of necessity to act offensively against the Turks.

On 15th January Admiral Duckworth, flying his flag in the *Royal George*, parted company with his chief, carrying instructions 'to proceed with his command as expeditiously as possible to the Straits of Constantinople, and there take up such position as would enable him to bombard the town, in case of refusal to give up the Turkish Fleet.' He was, however, to consult the Ambassador on the 'measures proper to be pursued', and it was only when the Ambassador was of the opinion that hostilities should commence, that the Admiral was to make a peremptory demand for the surrender of the Turkish Fleet.

Lord Collingwood stated: 'At this crisis, should any negotiations on the subject be proposed by the Turkish Government, as such proposition will probably be to gain time for preparing their resistance or securing their ships, I would recommend that no negotiations should continue for more than half an hour, and in the event of an absolute refusal, you are either to cannonade the town, or attack the Fleet wherever it may be, holding in mind that the getting possession, and next to that the destruction, of the Turkish Fleet is the object of the first consideration.'

Duckworth anchored off Tenedos on 10th February with eight sail of the line, including the *Canopus*—flying the flag of Rear-Admiral Sir Thomas Louis, and the *Pompe*—that of Rear-Admiral Sir Sydney Smith—two frigates and two bombships. Duckworth now learnt from Louis that some of the batteries in the Dardanelles were dilapidated, others partially mounted and poorly manned; and that the bulk of the Turkish Fleet lay moored in the Port of Constantinople, practically unequipped, except for a small squadron at anchor above the Narrows.

While waiting off the entrance of the Straits for a favourable wind, Duckworth wrote to Collingwood, pointing out all the dangers and hazards of the enterprise. Indeed it is clear that his heart was not in it from the outset.

On 19th February 1807, the wind having shifted to south-west,

Duckworth sailed up the Dardanelles, his squadron being led by Rear-Admiral Louis in the *Canopus*, the *Royal George*—flying Duckworth's flag—being the third ship in the line. The forts at the entrance opened fire; this was not replied to by the ships, at the suggestion of the Ambassador. However, as it was obvious that the Turks meant to resist the passage of the squadron, the forts at the Narrows were hotly engaged as the ships sailed by. The latter sustained only trifling damage and their casualties amounted to no more than 6 killed and 51 wounded.

The small Turkish squadron reported in the Straits, consisting of one 64-gun ship, four frigates, four corvettes, some brigs and gunboats, was anchored above Nagara Point on the Asiatic shore, and rashly opened fire on the ships as they passed, otherwise it seems probable that Duckworth would have spared it. One brig was allowed to escape, without being pursued, and thus Constantinople received warning of the successful passage of the Fleet. The remainder of the Turkish vessels, except one corvette which was captured, were destroyed under the guns of a redoubt mounting thirty-one heavy pieces, by the three ships in the rear of the line, and two frigates under command of Sir Sydney Smith; the redoubt was most gallantly carried by a landing party of blue-jackets and marines, who spiked the guns before withdrawing. Our losses in this engagement only amounted to 10 killed and 77 wounded.

Sir Sydney Smith, having detached the frigate *Active* and some of the boats of his ships to take possession of the prize and complete the destruction of the Turkish ships, rejoined Duckworth, who had anchored the remainder of his squadron about 3 miles above Nagara Point. Duckworth then weighed, and running up the Straits before a strong southerly breeze, entered the Marmora at 8 p.m. He reduced sail to such an extent during the night that little progress was made, and the wind falling light the next day, he did not arrive off Constantinople until 10 p.m. on 20th February, and then anchored off Prince's Island, 8 miles from the town.

On the 21st the wind was favourable for carrying out Collingwood's instructions, but Duckworth considered that he was still bound to act as directed by the Ambassador, in spite of the hostile reception he had received from the forts and ships in the Dardanelles.

The Ambassador then started a warfare of notes, conveying threats which were not carried into effect, and demands which were treated with utter contempt by the Turks. On the 22nd the Ambassador fell sick and the Admiral carried on the paper war single-handed.

Meanwhile the Turks were busily engaged equipping their ships and, under the direction of French engineers, energetically erecting batteries at every assailable point. On 27th February it was discovered that the Turks had occupied Prota Island, one of the Prince's Islands, and were erecting a battery abreast of our squadron. Rear-Admiral Louis asked permission to drive the Turks out of the island; Duckworth agreed, subject to the proviso, 'that no risks whatever were to be run, if it could be effected without hazarding the people, it might'. The *Canopus'* landing party was inadequate and suffered a check, and reinforcements were not permitted by Duckworth to do more than extricate their comrades. The casualties in this sorry affair were 7 killed and 19 wounded.

The wind from the 17th to 28th was favourable for finishing the business, in accordance with Collingwood's instructions, but the Fleet remained at anchor.

On 1st March the wind shifted to north-east, and Duckworth weighed and formed line of battle. The temper of the Rear-Admirals, and of the Fleet generally by this time, can well be imagined; everyone must have been spoiling to wipe out the humiliations of the past ten days. However, Duckworth had no intention of fighting, despite his threats, and after standing off and on all day, as he reported, to give the Turkish 'Fleet' (five ships of the line and four frigates), which were lying in the Roads, an opportunity to come out and attack him, he withdrew at nightfall and stood towards the Dardanelles, anchoring in the afternoon of 2nd March 6 miles above the Narrows. He was joined there by the *Active* and her prize; the latter by Duckworth's orders was restored to the prisoners.

On the morning of 3rd March Duckworth weighed and proceeded down channel; on approaching the Castle at the Narrows, hoping no doubt further to propitiate the Turks, Sir John fired a salute of thirteen guns. The salute was returned with shot and shell as the ships sailed by, again led by the *Canopus*. The casualties in the course of the withdrawal amounted to 29 killed and 138 wounded.

Duckworth was selected by the Admiralty because he was believed to be an officer possessing 'much ability and firmness', to quote their instructions to Lord Collingwood; but it sometimes happens in war that an officer, who is an able and excellent subordinate, falters under the stress of supreme responsibility.

Duckworth's pusillanimous irresolution from the outset doomed the enterprise to a humiliating failure.

On 8th February 1915 I was sent for by Mr Churchill (First Lord of the Admiralty) and told to leave the following day for Malta, to act as Chief of Staff to Admiral Carden, who was to command a Franco-British squadron destined to force the Dardanelles, occupy the Marmora, and demonstrate off Constantinople. I learnt that the Russians had begged us to make a diversion in that quarter, and that Lord Kitchener had asked Mr Churchill what the Navy could do to help, but had declared that he could not provide any troops to co-operate. Mr Churchill, appreciating the immense strategic possibilities, had undertaken with Lord Fisher's reluctant concurrence to attempt to force the Straits with old battleships, on the understanding that the attack would be broken off if the opposition was found to be too formidable.

A number of old battleships and cruisers were assembled at Malta ready for sea when I arrived there, and there was an atmosphere of excitement and anticipation in the air, but our destination was a closely guarded secret. When we sailed, it was given out that we were going to Naples and subsequently to Gibraltar, but when we were clear of the land, we steamed to the eastward, and on the morning of 19th February operations commenced to reduce the fortifications of Sedd-el-Bahr and Kum Kale, which guarded the entrance to the Dardanelles. We knew the calibre of all the guns in the forts, their ranges and the bearings on which they could fire; the plan of action was to open with deliberate long-range bombardment at anchor, either out of range or out of bearing of the enemy's guns. When their fire was reduced, the old ships were to run into very close range of the forts and smother them with the fire of their secondary 6 in. armaments. The action had to be broken off that afternoon for some days, owing to bad weather and low visibility, but it was renewed on the 25th, and after a tremendous bombardment the enemy abandoned these fortifications that evening. The following day demolition parties of bluejackets, covered by marines, were landed on either shore to complete the destruction of the guns, which was accomplished with the loss of one man killed and six wounded.

The success of this operation encouraged the Government to send out troops, which had been withheld when Mr Churchill first undertook to attempt to force the Straits by ships alone.

Then followed some disappointing delays, owing to the inefficiency of our mine-sweepers, and their inability to clear the minefields against the strong current which normally runs out of the Straits. Admiral Carden fell sick and was succeeded by Admiral de Robeck, who had laid the old ships alongside the forts with great gallantry. By 18th March the waters in which the Fleet was to mànœuvre, during the attack on the fortifications at the Narrows, were reported clear of mines, and that morning four French and five British battleships and a battle-cruiser steamed in to engage the forts. Eight British battleships remained outside, in readiness to move in when required.

According to a Turkish General Staff account, the situation in the forts was critical by 2 p.m. At that time four British battleships had just relieved the French ships, which had put up a great fight and were steaming out, when the old French battleship *Bouvet* blew up on a mine and most of her company perished. By 4 p.m. the forts at the Narrows were practically silenced, the batteries guarding the minefields were contained, no British ship had received any serious injury, and the situation appeared to be most favourable; it only remained for the mine-sweepers to play their part; but the crews of the trawler mine-sweepers, who would readily face any danger from mines, could not be induced to advance against the gun-fire, which by that time was really negligible.

We then lost two battleships sunk, and the battle-cruiser grievously injured, by mines, and the attack had to be abandoned.

It is true that our losses were heavy, but reinforcements were approaching, spirits were high, and, a fortnight after our reverse, a splendid mine-sweeping force of destroyers had been trained, and we were ready and eager to renew the attack; moreover, by then a considerable army had arrived and were waiting in transports, ready to exploit our success, if we achieved our object.

Throughout 18th March the utter contempt of death displayed by our destroyers and picket-boats was an inspiration and we felt that the new sweeping force would simply tear a way through the minefields and enable the ships to close to a range from which they would be able to pulverize the forts and batteries, as they did the outer forts on 25th February. In fact, we were confident that our destroyers and the obsolete battleships—which were useless in the main theatre of the North Sea—were on the threshold of winning imperishable fame.

However, Fate decided otherwise, and the naval attack was abandoned, at a moment when success seemed assured, in order not to jeopardize the execution of what was described as 'a bigger and better scheme', i.e., the landing of an army to capture the

Gallipoli Peninsula, in order to safeguard the Fleet's communications, after it had entered the Marmora.

I was very unhappy at the delay, which the change of plan en-
tailed, because I felt, after our experience on the 18th March, that
the enemy was beaten and that the Fleet could enter the Marmora
without serious loss, if it did so at once. The political issues and
what happened after we arrived in the Marmora were the
Government's concern—and if the Government were wrong, I did
not regard the withdrawal from the Marmora as a very dangerous
operation, as the minefields would have been swept, the ships
would have a strong favourable current, and we would be able
to attack the forts in reverse at short range. I felt therefore that the
naval attack alone was well worth the risk, to win so great a prize.

According to the Official Military History, the evidence is overwhelming that the Fleet's arrival off Constantinople would have
been decisive. Liman von Sanders, German Commander-in-Chief
of the Turkish Army, and the American Ambassador at Constantinople have placed on record that the fall of the Outer Forts
caused consternation in Turkey. Everyone in Constantinople believed that the success of the Allied Fleets was inevitable. Liman
von Sanders has stated (*Fünf Jahre Turkei*) that at the end of
February the Turkish Headquarters firmly believed that the
Straits would be forced. Everything had been prepared for the
departure of the Sultan and his court, as well as civil and military
authorities, to the interior of Asia Minor. These precautions, he
significantly adds, were justified.

It is important to realize that had Constantinople been abandoned, the Turks would have been unable to continue the war.
Their only arms and munition factories were at the capital and
would have been destroyed by the Fleet, and the supply of
material from Germany would have been impossible.

According to the German official account: 'Most of the
Turkish ammunition had been expended. The medium howitzers
and minefield batteries had fired half of their supply...between
30 to 50 rounds per gun.... Particularly serious was the fact that

the long range H.E. shells, which alone were effective against armour, were nearly used up. Fort Hamidieh had only 17 of them, Kilid Bahr but 10. Also there was no reserve of mines. What then was to happen if the battle was renewed on the 19th and following days with undiminished violence?'

We now had to prepare the stage for a combined naval and military attack on the Narrows. The Greek islands which we used as bases had no facilities for disembarking and re-sorting the various military units ready to land in the face of opposition, a consideration which had been overlooked when they were embarked in England. So all the transports had to be sent to Alexandria for the reorganization to be carried out.

Every available tug and lighter in the Mediterranean was taken up by the Navy and the battleships had to be almost demobilized to provide the crews for the innumerable small craft, required for disembarking this, the greatest amphibious expedition in the history of the world. Eventually the armada of some two hundred great vessels and hundreds of small craft assembled at Mudros, and at nightfall on 24th April it set out on its great adventure.

In the meantime the Turks had been digging and wiring with feverish haste, and we, who had seen a handful of seamen and marines land with trifling loss on 26th February, watched British and French soldiers, thanks to the long delay, suffer thousands of casualties in striving to take possession of the same positions two months later.

One had often heard it said that Sir Ian Hamilton ought to have landed at Bulair, but the object he was given was to enable the Fleet to enter the Marmora. The Bulair line was a veritable fortress, which would have had to be captured before the Army could have advanced down the Peninsula, to capture the heights and forts dominating the Narrows. The German ships *Goeben* and *Breslau* and Turkish battleships and destroyers would have been on his Eastern flank, he would have had a Turkish army to the northward of him, another to the south could have been reinforced from Asia Minor across the Straits. Meanwhile the British

Fleet would have been able to do little to help, unless it was prepared to force the Straits unaided, as originally intended.

His plan therefore was to land the 29th Division at the end of the Peninsula at Helles on three beaches ('V', 'W' and 'X'), and the Australian and New Zealand Army Corps (Anzacs) under General Birdwood at Gaba Tepe. There were to be two subsidiary landings, one in Morto Bay and the other on the western flank of the Peninsula at 'Y' Beach, which was about as difficult as that which Wolfe used to reach the Plains of Abraham. In fact this last landing was a naval suggestion, and as we hoped was unopposed. Two battalions and a company were landed there just before dawn and were unmolested all day, behind the enemy's defence line, they were actually stronger than the whole Turkish force in the southern part of the Peninsula; but they and the landing at Morto Bay, which secured its objective, also behind the enemy's defence line, remained inactive all day, waiting for the troops at the main landing to advance. In another subsidiary landing a small French force captured Kum Kale without much opposition, but as it was not possible to hold it, they were transferred to Gallipoli the following day.

The positions selected for the main landings at 'V' and 'W' were heavily wired and entrenched, and enfiladed by machine guns, screened from bombardment from the sea, the troops suffered very heavy losses and were held up all day at 'V' Beach, despite the heavy bombardment of high-explosive shells of 12 in. and 15 in. calibre, which apparently turned the whole Turkish position into an inferno.

Every effort was made to induce General Hunter Weston, who commanded the attack, to divert the reinforcements to the flank landings, but he would not alter his original plan. Two battalions of our troops were run ashore on 'V' Beach in an old collier, the *River Clyde*, which gave them some protection, but it was not until night fell that they were able to land a sufficient force to capture the position.

The Anzac landing was practically unopposed to start with, but was held up before it had made much progress.

Individual sailors had the honour of sharing in the perils of the assault, in the boats, in the *River Clyde*, and working on the beaches, but our Fleet had the intolerable ordeal of watching the Army's heroic effort and the desperate fighting in which even our guns could often take no part, owing to the proximity of friend and foe. The struggle for the capture of Krithia, Achi Baba, and the heights surrounding Anzac raged for several days, and at length on 8th May we learnt from the General that the Army was fought out, and at a complete deadlock; until large reinforcements and a liberal supply of ammunition arrived nothing further could be done, and this meant a delay of three or four weeks. On the other hand, we were assured that the power of defence under modern conditions had proved so greatly superior to that of attack, that the Army was confident of its ability to withstand any assault that the enemy might deliver.

It seemed to us that the moment had now arrived for the Navy to play its part. With the Army firmly established on shore, our losses replaced, and an efficient and dauntless mine-sweeping force, we were much better off, from a naval point of view, than we were on 19th March, when there had been no question of our not renewing the naval attack at the earliest possible moment.

On 9th May the Admiral telegraphed his readiness to attack, if ordered to do so. It is on record that Mr Churchill was anxious to give the necessary order and actually drafted a telegram, breathing confident encouragement. However, Lord Fisher was no longer ready to share the responsibility with him, and left the Admiralty. In the political upheaval which followed, Mr Churchill was superseded.

We were then told that the Navy's opportunity had passed, and that the Army would do the business. So the combined attack, for which the naval attack had been abandoned, was never delivered. The Fleet was not allowed to attack again; and yet, if every ship in the Allied squadron had been sunk with all hands in the Dardanelles, the naval losses would still have been less than half of those suffered in killed alone by the Army in Gallipoli, in its effort to help the Navy to force the Straits.

Deprived of Mr Churchill's vigorous direction and tireless energy, the campaign was again allowed to wilt and decline for several weeks, and the reinforcements and ammunition sent out from time to time barely filled the gaps caused by the incessant fighting and by sickness, which also took a heavy toll of the sorely tried troops.

At length the Government decided to prosecute the campaign vigorously, and by the end of July several new divisions, a fair supply of ammunition, and numbers of specially built motor-lighters arrived, to take part in a great offensive which was to be delivered early in August. The main object of the operation was to seize a position astride of the Peninsula, just above the Narrows. The attack was opened by the VIII Corps early in the afternoon of 6th August in the southern area, with the object of holding the enemy to their ground. Later, the same afternoon, the Anzac Corps, which had been reinforced secretly by about 25,000 men during the four previous nights, delivered an attack against the enemy's southern defence system in that sector, in order to draw his reserves away from the northern sector, where the main Anzac attack was to be launched against the Sari Bair Ridge, which over-looked the Narrows; simultaneously with the latter, two of the 'New Army' divisions (10th and 11th) were to seize Suvla Bay and operate on the northern flank of Anzac.

The diversion of the VIII Corps was a costly failure. By the morning of the 7th the enemy had decided that the risks must be accepted in the southern area, and withdrew a fresh division, which had been in reserve there, to reinforce the northern zone with all speed. The Australians and New Zealanders fought magnificently and on the afternoon of the 6th, after desperate hand-to-hand fighting, the 1st Australian Brigade established itself in a number of small posts in the heart of the Turkish position known as Lone Pine in the southern Anzac area, and they soon gained a complete ascendancy over the enemy in that zone.

The main Anzac attack was delivered by the New Zealand and Australian Division, the 13th Division of the New Army, and the Indian Infantry and Mountain Artillery Brigades. It was opened at 9 p.m. on the 6th by the New Zealand Mounted Rifles Brigade and two battalions of the 13th Division capturing important Turkish posts north of Anzac. The way was then clear for the advance on Chunuk Bair; but two assaulting columns, which had a very difficult route, went astray in the darkness, and when the attack was delivered, with the greatest gallantry, on the morning of the 7th, it was repulsed with heavy loss.

The landing of 10,000 men of the 11th Division, during the night of the 6th–7th, in Suvla Bay, and on the stretch of beach to the southward of it, completely surprised the enemy, but these troops and the 10th Division, which landed early on the 7th, failed to advance, despite the fact that for two days they were opposed by no more than 700 Gendarmerie, and the few guns which opened fire on them at daylight on the 7th were withdrawn before nightfall to avoid capture. When the long-delayed attack was delivered on the morning of the 9th, they then encountered the strong Turkish reinforcements which had been rushed 30 miles by forced marches from Bulair. The attack was then repulsed everywhere, and our troops in this zone were driven back to the positions from which they had started. The failure of these two divisions to exploit, during the first two days, the wonderful strategic opportunity of their surprise landing sealed the fate of the military effort.

Meanwhile, at Anzac, the battle for the Sari Bair Ridge was raging furiously. Here the young troops of the New Army, resolutely led, and imbued with the spirit of Anzac, fought splendidly. A New Zealand battalion captured Chunuk Bair at dawn on the 8th, and for a short time was able to look down on the waters of the Narrows. The crest, however, was untenable, but, with the assistance of two battalions of the 13th Division a valuable position on the south-west end of Chunuk Bair was held all day against fierce counter-attacks. Elsewhere the attack on the ridges had failed. It had been hoped that the advance from Suvla would greatly assist the Anzac attack, by threatening the Turkish northern flank; but it was soon evident that little help could be expected from the Suvla troops.

The general attack on the ridges was resumed on the 9th, and a battalion of Gurkhas captured Chunuk Bair and were also able to look down on the Narrows, but they were driven back by gun-fire, which was reported at the time to be British, but was after-wards proved to have been Turkish.

The brave atmosphere of Anzac, undaunted by its cruel losses and disappointments in the last three days, was something to be proud of; but, by midday on the 9th, the August offensive at Anzac had also failed, although the indomitable Anzacs would not admit it.

There is now overwhelming proof that our enemies were under no illusion as to the menace of the great strategic turning move-ment of the attack on the Dardanelles, which was initiated and pressed so vigorously by Mr Winston Churchill, to his undoing; and that neutral Powers, in their anxiety to be on the winning side, watched with intense interest and anxiety the progress of our effort, which, if successful, they knew would bring about the downfall of the Central Powers. While the Suvla landing was in progress, Admiral von Tirpitz wrote: 'The situation is obviously very critical. Should the Dardanelles fall, the World War has been decided against us.'

There is clear evidence to show that Falkenhayn—Chief of the German General Staff—had intended to overwhelm the British Army in France in the spring of 1915. However, alarmed at the Allied attack on the Dardanelles, and fearing that, if we forced the Straits, Bulgaria would come in on our side, he turned his atten-tion to the eastward, being confident that the German western front was strong enough to resist any Franco-British attack. After inflicting a heavy defeat on Russia, he proceeded to overrun Serbia, in order to open the road to Constantinople, instead of continuing the attack on Russia, as desired by the Austrians. 'It is incomparably more important', he wrote to the Austrian G.H.Q., 'that the Dardanelles should be secured, and in addition, the iron in Bulgaria struck while it is hot.'

Meanwhile, Bulgaria, which had been sitting on the fence waiting to see which side was likely to prove the victor, greatly impressed by the heavy Russian defeats and our Suvla failure, decided to back Germany, and proceeded to mobilize.

Bulgaria's threatened intervention brought about a tragic situation and completed the discomfiture of the military campaign in Gallipoli. Appealed to for help by Serbia, the French and British Governments decided to send troops to Salonika. Thus—at a moment when the Allied armies on the Western front were launching an attack (which was to suffer 250,000 casualties in a fruitless effort to break the German line) and could spare neither troops nor munitions for our enterprise, which was at a standstill for want of support—the Allied Governments embarked on yet another oversea campaign, which was only a drain on the Gallipoli army's inadequate resources.

Sir Ian Hamilton and his Chief of Staff, whose relations with Admiral de Robeck and myself were as close and friendly as those which existed between Wolfe and Saunders, were superseded; because when Sir Ian was asked to consider and prepare for evacuation, he declared it was unthinkable. General Sir Charles Munro and a new Chief of Staff came out, charged—my new colleague told me—'to put a stop to this damned side show'. The soldiers in power at home could not see beyond the barbed wire of the Western front, and killing Germans there, and did not realize that the result of taking our troops away from Gallipoli would free the Turkish Army to operate in Palestine and drive us out of Mesopotamia.

Meanwhile the campaign lingered on; Admiral de Robeck, who had borne the heat and burden of the day, went home for a rest, having acquiesced in the evacuation of Anzac and Suvla 'to shorten the line', at a council of war just before he sailed. The command was left in the hands of Admiral Wemyss. Repeated requests from him to be allowed to force the Straits were rejected. The originator of the project, who would have carried it through to a victorious issue, being no longer in the War Cabinet, had thrown up his Government office and was fighting in the trenches on the Western front, in command of a battalion. A MAN was wanted to make a decision, but those who bore the responsibility faltered under the conflicting advice given to them by soldiers and sailors, and, after weeks of indecision, eventually ordered the evacuation of Anzac and Suvla in December 1915, and of Helles in January 1916.

The evacuation of Suvla and Anzac was successful, because the enemy 'knew' that strong reinforcements had come out to the Eastern Mediterranean, and it did not occur to them to imagine that we could be so foolish as to start a new campaign elsewhere when we held all the trump cards in Gallipoli. Deserters surrendered every night; we know that the enemy expected to be attacked, and they were seen rolling out fresh wire the evening before the evacuation. We were indeed fortunate, for the weather broke a few hours after the last man left, and a gale destroyed all the piers and a number of lighters and boats, without which the evacuation could not have been carried out.

At Helles, on the day before the final evacuation took place, the enemy were heavily repulsed when they attempted to drive our troops into the sea. They knew we were going soon, but a gale was rising while the evacuation was taking place, and although they might have fired some thousands of shells on to the piers and beaches, they refrained from firing even the normal number, because they thought it too rough for our beach parties to carry out even the ordinary routine work.

For me, the Dardanelles Campaign is crowded with memories. The heroic spirit of the 29th Division, ·which entered into the soul of every new draft and prevailed to the end. The fighting ardour of the Anzacs, which was simply unquenchable. The bravery of the New Army and the Territorials and Yeomen, who fought like veterans; and, above all, the patient endurance of all the men, through the summer heat, flies and pestilence, which were followed by winter gales, blizzards, and frost-bite.

The indomitable enterprise of the submarines, which dived through treacherous currents, under minefields, and crashed through the net defences in the Straits, to operate on the enemy's lines of communication in the Marmora.

The excellent work of the naval beach parties and of those who manned the small craft that supplied the Army, continually under fire throughout the campaign. On the last and most anxious night of all, when the beaches were lashed with breaking waves, and lighters and boats were crashing against the fragile piers and stagings, a disaster was only averted by the skill and devotion of the officers and men working on the beaches and manning the troop-carriers, trawlers and drifters, lighters and boats, which embarked guns, animals, and men under incredibly difficult conditions. Finally, the admirable seamanship displayed by the destroyer captains, who manœuvred their frail vessels in pitch darkness on a lee shore, in order to embark the rear-guard of 6000 men practically simultaneously from alongside the *River Clyde* and the hulks, which had been sunk to act as breakwaters.

The following is from a letter I wrote at the time: 'At 3.55 a.m., to our intense relief, bonfires were lit, which meant that the last man had left the shore. Five minutes later our store dumps were in a colossal blaze. At last the enemy realized that we were really going, scores of rockets shot into the sky from Asia and Gallipoli. Every enemy gun burst into flame, and the beaches and piers, which half an hour before were crowded with men, were smothered with bursting shells. Our ammunition dumps all over the Peninsula, exploded by time fuses, contributed to the confusion; finally our main magazine blew up with a terrific roar. Then the enemy realized that we had gone. But I think that they had every right to consider that the evacuation of the whole army, which had withstood their attack on the previous day, should have been a physical impossibility on that stormy night. The only casualty was one bluejacket, killed by a piece of falling debris, as the last boat plunged her way to seaward in the teeth of what was, by that time, a sou' westerly gale.'

These are memories which one can recall with pride and satis-faction, but there are also tormenting memories, which are recorded as follows in my *Naval Memoirs*:

'I was present when the first shot of the campaign was fired in February, 1915, and the last in January, 1916, and during all the intermediate fighting, serving as Chief-of-Staff to the three admirals, who successively commanded the naval operations. I spent many hours in the Dardanelles under fire from the forts and concealed howitzers—a greatly exaggerated menace. I saw ships sink by mine and torpedo, watched the Homeric fighting on the beaches, and the great battles which followed, in the course of which thousands of soldiers perished.

'I lived in close association with the administrative officers at the advanced bases, and the fighting soldiers in Gallipoli. I watched and helped in the organisation of three unopposed evacuations.

'I wish to place on record that I had no doubt then, and have none now—and nothing will ever shake my opinion—that from the 4th April, 1915, onwards, the Fleet could have forced the Straits, and with losses trifling in comparison with those the army suffered; could have entered the Marmora with sufficient force to destroy the Turko-German fleet.

'This operation would have cut the communications—which were sea-borne—of any Turkish armies, either in Gallipoli or on the Asiatic side, and would have led immediately to a victory, decisive upon the whole course of the war.'

The lessons of Quebec, China, and Gallipoli stand out in history, but it seems inevitable that each successive generation must needs learn the same lessons over again by trial and error.

The landings at 'Y' Beach and Morto Bay were endeavours to profit by the example set by Wolfe at Foulon, under the Plains of Abraham. They also took the enemy completely by surprise, and he had no troops available to counter them, but unfortunately they were not exploited, and our failure to do so was one of the principal causes of our ultimate defeat.

When Wolfe was held up in his attack on Beauport, he did not throw in more troops, which would only have become involved in the same difficulties, but he wisely withdrew them, making use of sea power to make an attack elsewhere with successful results.

In the early days in Gallipoli, reserves were often used and dissipated in vain efforts to carry through attacks which were hopelessly held up, rather than making use of them to exploit successes elsewhere.

There was a moment when the dominant key point—Achi Baba hill—was almost within our reach; a Lancashire Territorial Brigade was on its slopes, within 100 yards of its summit, but it was left unsupported, all the available reserves having been expended in trying to force through an attack to the westward of that coveted prize. That was a tragic failure with far-reaching results.

Admiral de Robeck had declared that he would renew the naval attack on the Narrows, directly an observation post had been established to direct the fire of the ships, our few and primitive aircraft of those days being incapable of doing so for long for the large fleet engaged. With Achi Baba in our hands, the combined naval and military operation, for which we were waiting, could hardly have been avoided.

Much has been said by critics of the Gallipoli Campaign about the ineffectiveness of naval gunfire to assist land operations, which is not borne out by evidence; although it was painfully evident to all who witnessed the heroic efforts to storm 'V' Beach, which were held up by three or four well-sited machine-guns, despite the fact that the Turkish position had been turned into an inferno by naval 12 in. and 15 in. high-explosive shells. On the other hand, Turkish official documents all agree as to the shattering moral effect of the ships' guns, so much so that the Turkish Commander on one occasion recommended retirement. However,

Liman von Sanders vetoed this, and declared that: 'The best way to get cover from the British ships is to advance, rather than retire, and to establish the line as close as possible to the Allied trenches.'

An excellent maxim, equally valuable nowadays, when subjected to heavy bombardment from the air.

Among the most valuable lessons we learnt from the original landings was the folly of attempting to storm a defended beach in daylight. All our amphibious operations after this, whether attacking or evacuating, were carried out with as many hours of darkness in hand as was possible, and also, having regard to the vital importance of surprise, doing nothing to disclose our intentions before dark.

Later in the war, I had the good fortune to be given an opportunity of putting into practice the lessons I had learned when, on 1st January 1918, I was given command of the Dover Patrol with an absolutely free hand to make war on the Belgian Coast.

For this I have to thank the First Sea Lord—Admiral Sir Rosslyn Wemys—the third Admiral under whom I served at the Dardanelles, who, before the evacuation, made such strenuous efforts to be allowed to launch a combined naval and military operation, which would most surely have carried that campaign to a successful conclusion.

CHAPTER IV

COMBINED OPERATIONS ON THE
BELGIAN COAST, 1918

(See Maps VII and VIII, pp. 109, 110)

Towards the end of September 1917, much to my disgust, I had been brought down from the Grand Fleet, where I was a Rear-Admiral in command of a division of battleships, to be the first Director of Plans at the Admiralty.

At that time our submarine losses were enormous, and the Admiralty considered that it was absolutely essential to capture the submarine base at Bruges, if we were to be able to continue the war; and in consequence of their representations to the War Cabinet, a great military offensive was launched to capture the Belgian ports. After suffering terrible losses it was held up in the mud and slime of the Passchendaele Ridge.

Despite the heavy shipping losses in the western approaches and the western part of the Channel, the Admiral at Dover maintained that a mined net from the Downs to the Belgian Coast denied the passage of the Straits, and the fact that no submarine attacks were delivered in the eastern part of the Channel gave substance to his claim.

Fortunately, however, a German submarine, which was sunk off Waterford Harbour, provided most valuable information, including the following instructions given to submarines for passing through the Straits of Dover:

'It is best to pass the Dover net defences on the surface; if forced to dive, go down to 40 metres. As far as possible go as far as Cherbourg without being observed. On the other hand, the boats, which in exceptional cases pass round Scotland, are to let themselves be seen as freely as possible in order to mislead the English.'

The submarine also contained information of the number of

submarines which had passed through the Straits, and it was clear
that they were passing through at the rate of over 30 a month.

We then made out plans for defeating the submarines by laying
an enormous deep minefield between Folkestone and the French
coast, patrolling it with trawlers and drifters, supported by
destroyers and monitors night and day. At night it was illuminated by flares, which would turn that strip of the Channel into
a glare of light.

We recommended that the mined net should be abandoned and
an attempt made to block Zeebrugge and Ostend, the exits of the
canals connecting those ports with the submarine base at Bruges.

Owing to difficulties in getting these plans put into execution,
I was told to carry them out myself and take over the Dover
command.

On 1st January 1918 I was appointed Acting Vice-Admiral
Commanding the Dover Patrol and had under my command
some 300 vessels, including large and small monitors, a light
cruiser, flotilla leaders, destroyers, P-boats, trawlers, drifters,
mine-sweepers, M.L.s, C.M.B.s and submarines. My command
included a number of naval guns, 12 in., 9·2 in. and 7·5 in.,
manned by marines and seamen, mounted in batteries behind the
Belgian lines, also fifteen squadrons of the R.N.A.S., day and
night bombers and fighters, based on aerodromes westward of
Dunkirk, with a landing ground at Dover, where I kept an aircraft which I used like a motor car to take me all over my command and to visit the Military H.Q.s of Sir Douglas Haig, who
told me that he looked upon my command as the left flank of the
Allied Army. The Belgian Army rested on the sea and my
monitors, siege guns and aircraft co-operated with them. King
Albert and his Queen lived in a little villa amongst the sand dunes
at La Panne, which was actually within range of the German guns
near Nieuport.

The activities of the Dover Patrol were immense, and an
enormous organization carried out its daily duties with great
regularity and efficiency. For instance, the channels along the

coast from Dungeness to the Downs and to the French ports were swept by mine-sweepers every morning, before the transports and trade passed through them.

Troop-carriers which carried drafts and leave parties between Folkestone and Boulogne were each escorted by two destroyers, as were the hospital ships between Calais and Dover. The daily task was certainly arduous and efficiently carried out, but it was not making war.

I learnt from the Commanding Officers that the 12 in. monitors had not fired their guns for a year, because they were outranged by the enemy's fortress guns; that the attacks of our aircraft were restricted because of the fear of retaliation. On the other hand the enemy had refrained from provoking the Patrol for the last nine months. Their destroyers had resisted the temptation of destroying our anti-submarine net-barrage, although there was nothing to prevent them doing so, and we knew from the Waterford submarine that they were forbidden to attack vessels within the Dover Patrol area.

Thousands of our soldiers were fighting desperately in other areas, and I was determined that the Army should not be asked again to make sacrifices, in order to relieve the Navy from carrying out an operation which, cost what it might, would greatly handicap the enemy's submarine campaign, and I felt that a decision must now be fought for in the area confided to my charge.

I had learnt my lesson off Gallipoli, where I had watched a campaign that had infinite possibilities peter out through irresolution; and I was determined to put an end to the peaceful inaction in the Dover Straits for which our shipping farther afield was paying so heavily.

The maintenance of the mine net defence which ran across the Channel from the Downs to the Belgian coast had occupied the crews of nearly 100 drifters. It was left alone and the drifters were freed to patrol above the deep minefield which was laid, and increased continually, as mines became available. Being within close reach of a powerful destroyer force at Zeebrugge, it invited attack, which was not long in coming, and several patrol craft suffered heavily, but the patrol went on and many German submarines perished, being driven down on to the mines when they tried to go through on the surface.

Meanwhile, preparations to deliver a combined operation with all the forces under my command were pressed on. I was anxious to carry out this operation entirely with Naval and Marine personnel, and asked the Admiralty to make up a battalion of marines to act as assault troops, and was given a company 250 strong from each of the three Marine Depots, which assembled at Deal to receive battle training for the task before them.

I asked Sir David Beatty to lend me 300 bluejackets from the Grand Fleet to take part in the operation. These were drawn from every battleship and battle-cruiser, officers being selected by the Admirals of the Squadrons and told to select their own men who were likely to enjoy a hazardous operation. Later Admiral Beatty sent me stokers and E.R.A.s and Royal Marine Artillerymen, thus every branch of H.M. sea service was represented in our enterprise, the main objects of which were to block the Bruges ship-canal at its entrance into the harbour at Zeebrugge; to block the entrance to Ostend harbour from the sea; and to inflict as much damage as possible upon the ports of Zeebrugge and Ostend.

Zeebrugge harbour is connected by a ship-canal with the inland docks at Bruges, which communicates again by means of a system of smaller canals with Ostend harbour. The whole forms a triangle with two sea entrances. The eastern side, which is 8 miles long, is the ship-canal from Zeebrugge to Bruges; the southern side, which is 11 miles long, consists of smaller canals from Bruges to Ostend; the base, facing north-west, is the 12 miles of heavily fortified coast line between Ostend and Zeebrugge. This fortified line was prolonged 8½ miles to the westward, extending to the right flank of the German Army facing Nieuport, and 7 miles to the eastward as far as the Dutch frontier. The defences included a number of batteries mounting over 225 guns, 136 of which were from 6 in. to 15 in. calibre, the latter ranging up to 42,000 yards (23 miles).

This formidable system had been installed since the German occupation in 1914, and Bruges had provided a base for at least thirty-five enemy torpedo craft and about thirty submarines. By reason of its position and comparative security, it had constituted a continual and ever-increasing menace to the sea communications of our Army and the sea-borne trade and food supplies of the United Kingdom.

When the combined operations of the 22nd–23rd April were undertaken, it was believed that, although the blocking of the Zeebrugge entrance to the Bruges ship-canal was the most important of all objects, it would be necessary also to block the entrance to Ostend harbour, in order to seal up the Bruges ship-canal and docks; for unless this was done the lighter craft would still be able to pass to and fro more or less freely through the smaller canals.

The entrance to the Bruges canal at Zeebrugge was covered by a massive stone Mole, more than a mile long and 100 yards wide, on which was a railway station, the terminus of a line which linked the sea port of Bruges—Zeebrugge—with the Continental railway system. At that time, the Mole was connected with the shore by a steel viaduct, 300 yards long and 40 feet wide, and the tide raced through its piers.

A battery of quick-firing 4 in. guns at the end of the Mole would have to be passed, at a range of less than 100 yards, by blockships attempting to reach the canal entrance; it was important therefore to try and capture this battery before the blockships arrived.

It was important also, that while the Assaulting Force was engaged on the Mole, no reinforcements should arrive from the shore, and it was hoped to prevent this by running an old submarine, carrying 5 tons of high explosive, into the steel viaduct and blow a breach in it, thus turning the Mole into an island.

To get the ships carrying the Assaulting Force alongside the Mole and the blockships into the canal entrance, in the face of the formidable gunfire they would encounter, it was necessary to provide a smoke-screen to cover their approach; it was also necessary to carry out the blocking operation at high water and as near midnight as possible, in order to approach and leave the enemy's coast in darkness. If we could hit off this condition on a fine night, with a smooth sea and a light northerly wind, blowing the smoke-screen like a sea fog towards the shore, we hoped it would be possible to get the blockships and assaulting ships quite close to their objective before they were discovered.

If at the same time the enemy's attention could be diverted, by a tremendous bombardment from our heavily armed monitors, and if an air attack, from the splendid Naval Air Service attached to the Dover Patrol, could be delivered on the Mole, a few minutes before the Assaulting Force arrived, in order to drive the garrison of the Mole down inside their bomb-proof shelters, it might be possible to spring a complete surprise on the enemy.

In order to accustom the enemy to our appearance off the Belgian coast at night, the monitors bombarded and air attacks were made, while C.M.B.s (fast motor torpedo boats) were active off Zeebrugge and Ostend every favourable night.

It will be appreciated that our ability to operate at all in that heavily fortified area would depend entirely on an effective smoke-screen, to cover our approach until we were at close quarters. The only means of making smoke at that time was to burn sulphur in iron pots, which made a dense white smoke, but also a bright flame, which it had been found impossible to baffle; this, of course, was useless for a night operation dependent on surprise. The only other method was to make dense black smoke from the funnels of ships.

As the Germans used most effective smoke-screens, under cover of which they manœuvred to escape at the Battle of Jutland, I called in the aid of Wing-Commander Brock of the R.N.A.S. Experimental Station—one of the firework family of Crystal

Palace fame. He had invented an incendiary bullet, which was responsible for destroying several Zeppelins, and the brilliant flares, which were playing a vitally important part in illuminating our deep minefield anti-submarine barrage at Dover. Brock soon produced an excellent smoke by introducing chlor-sulphonic acid into the exhausts of the internal combustion engines of motor launches and C.M.B.s, and the funnels of destroyers.

The production of chlor-sulphonic acid was limited and much was being used in the manufacture of Saxine—a substitute for sugar.

I had originally hoped to carry out the operation in March, but I found it impossible to get enough smoke for the 130 vessels engaged until the War Cabinet gave orders that the manufacture of Saxine was to be completely shut down until all the chlor-sulphonic I needed had been delivered at Dover. This was not until early in April.

Brock's contribution to the undertaking was of great value to me, for in addition to fitting out the vessels with smoke-making apparatus, he designed special smoke-making floats, to be anchored in selected positions; he also designed immense flame-throwers for the assaulting ship; parachute flares for aircraft to drop; flare rockets for surface vessels to fire, and special light buoys to mark the route. Brock's one plea—which I would have preferred to refuse, as his genius for inventions was so valuable— was that he should be allowed to take part in the attack. He was particularly anxious to get on to the Mole, in order to find out the German method of sound ranging, so I reluctantly consented to his going with the Assaulting Force.

In the Dardanelles Campaign Naval Surveying officers had made bombarding charts, erected guiding marks on shore and laid buoys off the coast, which enabled ships to carry out accurately the bombardment of any object or area within their range, at the request of the Army. I obtained the services of these same officers and they made arrangements to lay Brock's light buoys, after dark, for the bombarding ships, and to mark the routes, to ensure correct timing, on which the whole plan of action depended.

I was given six old cruisers, including the *Vindictive*, to act as blockships. I thought the most suitable assault ship would be a fast handy shallow draft vessel with high freeboard, stoutly built to go alongside quays, such as those running between Holyhead and Queenstown. But I was told that nothing of the sort could be spared, so I decided to fit out the *Vindictive* for the purpose. Her draft was against her and she could hardly hope to escape hitting a mine, if we ran into a minefield; so I sent an officer round the ports to look for a couple of ferry-boats of the type one had so often seen bumping or ramming their bows up against a quay to nose themselves round in a tideway, and eventually selected two Mersey ferry-boats, the *Iris* and *Daffodil*. They could each carry about 1000 people, had double hulls and only drew about 11 feet of water. They could thus pass safely over any minefield round about high water.

Each blockship was fitted with two control positions well protected with defensive mats to keep out machine-gun and rifle fire. The three foremost guns remained to engage the batteries and defend the ship. Protection was given to machinery, boilers, etc. by concrete blocks. Charges were fitted for blowing out portions of the ships' bottoms with firing keys in each control position. An expert of the Liverpool Salvage Company was consulted and cement blocks and bags of cement were placed in positions to prevent or delay salvage, or the cutting away of a portion of the hull to free a passage. (After the war, the same Salvage Company took more than a year to move the two blockships out of the canal.)

In order to launch the assault from the *Vindictive* as nearly as possible from the level of the Mole parapet, a stout deck was built on the skid beams—on which the boats normally rested— from the fo'castle to the quarter-deck on the port side, the boat crutches being removed; three wide ramps sloped up from the starboard side of the upper deck to the false deck, to give ready access to it by the Assaulting Force, who would remain under cover as long as possible. Eighteen brows, or gangways, were hinged on the false deck and triced up, ready to be dropped on the parapet of the Mole, which, during the possible hours of attack, would be from 4 to 7 feet higher than the false deck.

In addition to her main armament, the *Vindictive* was provided with a 7·5 in. howitzer on her fo'castle, another on her false deck, and an 11 in. howitzer on her quarter-deck for engaging the batteries on shore and for firing at the lock gates of the canal.

Two large flame-throwers were mounted in shelters, one abreast of the fore bridge and the other at the after end of the upper deck. Pom-poms, Lewis guns and Stokes mortars were mounted along the port side. Three pom-poms and six Lewis guns were mounted in the foretop to fire over the parapet and cover the assault. The foremast above the top was removed. The mainmast was removed and laid horizontally across the quarter-deck, the heel was embedded in concrete and the end extended several feet beyond the ship's side, to act as a bumpkin to protect the port propeller. Special fenders were fitted to the port side to protect the ship's side from the underwater projection of the Mole, and huge fenders were fitted to the port side of the fo'castle to take the first bump when she went alongside.

It was rather fortunate that in October 1914 I happened to have spent three days alongside the Mole in a destroyer, while landing the 7th Division, and although we had detailed plans of the Mole, lock gates, etc. from the Belgian engineers who had built them, and who were refugees in Paris, the local knowledge I acquired then was of great value.

My first intention was to ram all the three blockships into the lock, if it was open—as seemed likely at high water with a bombardment in progress—and to sink one ship on each sill, but the depth of water at low spring tides in the lock and its vicinity, where there was no silt, was 19 feet, with a rise and fall of 14 feet. I was advised that it would be possible at low water to cut away sufficient of the blockships to allow a submarine, or even a destroyer, to pass over at high water. Lying in such a narrow channel, it would also be easy to build coffer-dams to dry dock the blockships, and rig shears over them to facilitate the work of removing the obstruction.

On the other hand aerial photographs showed an immense accumulation of silt at the entrance to the canal, and two Belgians, who had escaped from the Zeebrugge dredger, told us that the depth at the entrance to the canal was so reduced that even small submarines were unable to pass through the Channel at low tide. They declared that the trouble arising from silt at Zeebrugge was a very serious matter.

I decided therefore to sink the blockships at the entrance to the canal, since with the assistance of silt, it seemed likely to form a more permanent obstacle. However I hated giving up my project of sinking a ship in the lock entrance—if the gate was open— or ramming the lock gate, and decided that the leading ship should do so; a far easier task, once the canal was entered, than swinging the two ships into exactly the right positions across it. If only two ships succeeded in getting into the canal, they would have to concentrate on blocking the channel at the entrance.

Two submarines were fitted out to blow up the viaduct, in case one was unable to reach it. A charge of five tons of high explosive was put in the bows with two or three alternatives for exploding it. To enable the submarines to be abandoned before colliding with the viaduct, a gyro-control was fitted, which would hold the submarine on a steady course when the right position was reached. Motor dinghys were towed from a boom projecting from either side of the submarine for the crew to escape in, when it was set on the required course and the fuses started. A picket boat was provided to follow the submarine and pick up the crew.

Meanwhile the training of the Marine Light Infantry battalion went on at Deal, that of the seamen at Chatham, and the Marine Artillerymen were given instruction in the working of howitzers and pom-poms at Shoeburyness. A lay-out of Zeebrugge Mole was made on King's Down near Deal, the officers and men were told that it was a position in France which they would be called upon to attack, and attack it they did, vigorously by night and day. Both bluejackets and marines were given instruction in trench warfare and close fighting with bomb and bayonet, as well as Lewis gun and rifle.

It was necessary to provide some form of camouflage for all this activity at Dover, Chatham and Deal; I suggested that a letter should be sent to me from the Admiralty, marked 'Most Secret', copies of which I sent to the Commanders-in-Chief and other authorities, but 'inadvertently' I omitted the usual precautions which should have been taken when forwarding such a letter. The letter of 4th March was as follows:

'In view of the possibility of the enemy breaking through the line on the North Coast of France and attacking Calais and Dunkirk, a special battalion of Marines and a company of blue-jackets will be placed at your disposal for reinforcements, and to act as demolition parties etc. to destroy guns and stores. You are to make every preparation for blocking Calais and Dunkirk harbours at the last possible moment, with the ships whose names have been given you verbally, so as to deny the use of these ports to the enemy if necessary.'

This story got about as a great secret, and the enemy's March offensive gave colour to it.

On 3rd April the six old cruisers—*Vindictive, Thetis, Intrepid, Iphigenia, Sirius* and *Brilliant*—joined the old battleship *Hindustan* —which was used as a mother ship to house some of the men of the crowded ships—in the Swin, where they were joined by the two ferry-boats *Iris* and *Daffodil*.

On 6th April the 4th Battalion of Marines embarked in a transport at Dover 'bound for France', but when well clear of the land, course was altered for the Swin, where the men were transferred to the *Iris* and *Daffodil*.

In the Swin—an anchorage in the Thames Estuary—the ships were out of sight of land, and the only correspondence allowed was by active service postcards. I went to the Swin the next day and visited all the ships and spoke to the assembled ship's companies and told them the real object of the training they had

undergone. If any of them had any reason for wishing to withdraw, they could do so, and no one would think any the worse of
them. However, no one showed any sign of anything but enthusiasm and they cheered vigorously.

The total striking force numbered 142 vessels (excluding 23 of
the Harwich force, which, under the command of Commodore
Tyrwhitt, were to cruise to the northward to prevent any inter-
ference from enemy ships coming from the Heligoland Bight).

In addition to the 8 ships in the Swin, 74 vessels were working
from Dover and 60 from Dunkirk (including 7 French torpedo
craft) carrying out the ordinary duties of the Dover Patrol.

I confided the command of the attack on Ostend to Commodore Lynes—who commanded my advanced base at Dunkirk
—and I intended to lead the attack on Zeebrugge myself, flying
my flag in H.M.S. *Warwick*—a destroyer.

On 9th and 10th April, the first two of the five possible days of
the moonless period, the weather was unsuitable; on the 11th the
meteorological report was promising and our Armada put to sea.

The plan had been worked out on an exact time table for each
of the five possible days, and on this day we should have arrived
at Zeebrugge at 2.5 a.m., which would give time to do the
business and get well clear and out of range before dawn.

There was a gentle north-easterly wind and the sea was smooth;
but when we were only about 16 miles from our objective, the
wind dropped, shifted and blew offshore. I knew that it would be
suicidal to approach the coast unscreened by smoke, and I went
through a pretty difficult and trying time during the next few
moments, as it was essential to make a decision immediately.
I was terribly tempted, it would be so much easier to go on, and
trust to the God of Battles and the good fortune of the Navy, for
a happy issue. However, the wind being definitely against us,
I made the fateful signal, one word on the wireless, which cancelled the proceedings for the night.

As my flagship—the destroyer *Warwick*—lay stopped, while
I watched the Armada turn homewards, I had a reminder of the

power of the defences we had been about to challenge; a salvo of great shells came roaring from the shore, and pitched some 200 yards from the *Warwick* with a tremendous splash; evidently fired by the four 12 in. guns from Knocke, 32,000 yards away, obviously as a result of my signal.

On 13th April, the last possible day of the moonless period, we set out again, but it came on to blow very hard and was too rough for the small craft, so once again we had to return.

There was nothing to be done now, except hope for the best and wait for the next period in the following lunar month; but the following day, the First Sea Lord arrived at Dover; he commiserated with me on our bad luck, commended me for my prudence in returning, and told me that the Admiralty had decided that the expedition must be cancelled; as it could no longer be a surprise, the news would be certain to reach Germany, during the three weeks which must elapse before I could renew my attack. However, I told him that it would be high water about midnight in ten days' time—although the moon would be full—and I persuaded him to let me have another try then.

The 22nd April was the first possible day of the full moon period and the weather report was not too bad, and though it might have been better, the period might well pass without a more favourable opportunity, so I made the preparatory signal, which put the whole enterprise in motion once more.

My wife walked down the pier with me to see me off, she alone knew what a hell of a time I had been going through, and her last words were that the next day was St George's Day—he was certain to bring good fortune to our expedition, and she begged me to use 'St George for England' as our battle cry.

At 5 p.m. seventy-five vessels joined my flag—flying in the destroyer *Warwick*—and we set out on our adventure. Before night fell, I made a general signal—'St George for England'.

As we approached Zeebrugge, the *Warwick*, followed by the destroyers *North Star* and *Phoebe*, drew ahead, to drive off any enemy destroyers which might be patrolling off the port; we then remained close to the Mole, to protect the boarding vessels whilst they were alongside it.

Motor launches, supported by other destroyers, went to their allotted places to make the smoke-screen, and C.M.B.s tore backwards and forwards across our front, laying the first line of smoke to cover our advance.

The whole operation was governed by a time table, which was strictly adhered to, with one unfortunate exception; a misty drizzle, which started about an hour before we arrived, prevented the aircraft finding and delivering their attack on the Mole, and when the *Vindictive* arrived, a few seconds after midnight, the garrison was alert and at their guns, and the smoke being blown back at the last moment, the assaulting force suffered heavily from shell fire, as she went alongside, and her Captain went through a very trying time.

Aerial photographs had clearly shown a fortified zone about 150 yards from the end of the Mole, protecting the battery from a land attack. It was therefore my intention to lay the *Vindictive* alongside the Mole, as near as possible to the guns, which were on the extension. The bluejackets were to storm the guns and the marines attack the fortified position from inside. They were then to advance down the Mole, covering a force of bluejackets with demolition charges.

Unfortunately the *Vindictive* went on too far, and was eventually berthed—with the assistance of the *Daffodil*—340 yards beyond her planned position, and although the assault was carried out with the greatest gallantry, the attacking force was unable to capture the guns, as they were held up by the wire and machine-guns of the fortified zone, which was now between them and the guns at the end of the Mole.

The *Daffodil* played an invaluable part, by pushing the *Vindictive* alongside the Mole, and keeping her there throughout the action.

The *Iris* was unable to secure herself alongside the Mole, in spite of the heroic efforts of two young officers, who were killed on the parapet, while attempting to place her grappling anchors.

As the leading blockship, the *Thetis*, passed the end of the Mole, at the appointed time, bound for the lock gates of the canal—which she was to ram—she came under a devastating fire from the uncaptured Mole end battery, and sank before she reached the canal entrance.

The *Intrepid* and *Iphigenia*, however, were successfully sunk across the canal in their allotted positions.

Four motor launches had been detailed to follow the blockships in, to rescue the crews if possible. One was sunk, one broke down, one saved the survivors of the *Thetis*, and the fourth—'M.L. 282' —saved the crews of both the other blockships, in spite of tremendous machine-gun fire from the banks of the canal, which caused many casualties.

One submarine failed to arrive in time, owing to her tow parting, but the other, 'C. 3', rammed the Mole viaduct most successfully and blew a 100 foot gap in it; her gallant crew of two officers and four men disdained to make use of the gyroscopic gear and did not abandon their vessel until she was firmly wedged between the piers of the viaduct. They then escaped in their motor skiff, which was riddled with machine-gun bullets, and in a sinking condition, the motor being smashed, they had to row hard to get far enough away from the explosion of the submarine. The Captain and three men were badly wounded, when picked up by the rescuing picket-boat, which was commanded by the Captain's brother.

The *North Star* was sunk by gunfire, when she emerged from the smoke, but most of her crew were saved by the *Phoebe*.

Having seen the blockships in the canal entrance, and watched the safe withdrawal of the *Vindictive* from the Mole, I returned in the *Warwick* to the entrance of the harbour to look for the rescue motor launches, and was fortunate enough to meet 'M.L. 282' struggling out, simply packed with men from the *Intrepid* and *Iphigenia*, who stood up and cheered wildly, when they saw the

Warwick. I told them to come alongside, and 101 men were counted out—including a good many killed and 20 odd wounded. I doubt if she would have been licensed to carry fifty passengers in the calm waters of the Thames.

Some things that night stand out in my memory. The amazing brilliance of the enemy's star shells, which turned night into day.

The efficiency of our smoke-screens, which hid us in safety, until we had almost reached our objectives; then when at length the enemy became thoroughly alarmed, the roar with which great shells passed over our heads like express trains, when the enemy's batteries, still unable to see us, put down a tremendous barrage, which, fortunately for us, plunged harmlessly into the sea some miles behind us.

The great flame which shot into the sky and told us that the submarine had done her task, although we could not distinguish the sound of the explosion in the roar of the battle.

The intense relief I felt, when I knew that the battle was joined, and that there could be no more turning back, and that the issue then lay with the men and the young officers who led them so bravely.

Their courage and cool contempt of death struck a great blow which cheered our country in one of its blackest hours.

A good many conflicting stories have been told about the actual effect the operation had on the submarine campaign from the Flanders bases. The Germans of course belittled our effort and declared that a certain flotilla of torpedo boats and a U.B. submarine had passed out at high water. But these were very small shallow draught vessels, and as there was a rise of tide of 14 feet, they could actually pass over the sloping side of the canal, which was dry at low water, under the sterns of the blockships. Nevertheless week after week aerial photographs showed 12 destroyers, 11 torpedo boats and seven large submarines lying in the canals near Bruges, and it could be reasonably assumed that at least 12 more submarines were lying in the massive submarine shelters which gave them protection from our air raids.

At first these vessels were all lying in the basin at Bruges, and in the aerial photographs they looked like salmon in a pool waiting for a spate. After a few air raids, however, they were dispersed along the canals, a very popular berth being alongside a building marked with an enormous red cross painted on a white circle. A photograph taken on 15th June showed no change and there can be no question that up to that date, at any rate, the passage was blocked to all but very small craft. Photographs then showed that the Germans had removed two piers on the western bank and cut a passage through the silt under the sterns of the two blockships.

When I visited Zeebrugge in October 1918 this channel was almost dry at low water and was marked by great iron girders, through which vessels could only be warped at high water—a very laborious proceeding.

A further indication that Bruges harbour was successfully blocked was shown by the arrival of nine destroyers from the Heligoland Bight, which remained in the outer harbour of Zeebrugge and operated from there. We learnt too that submarines from one of the Flanders Flotillas—who were evidently out—were transferred and operated from the Heligoland Bight, after they returned from their cruises. I shall never cease to regret, however, that I did not adhere to my original intention of sinking all the blockships in the lock entrance. Judging by the difficulty experienced by the Liverpool Salvage Company in raising the *Iphigenia* and *Intrepid*, I am certain they would have absolutely blocked the Bruges canal for the duration of the war.

At Ostend, owing to the shifting of a buoy by the Germans, the blockships missed the entrance and ran ashore to the eastward of the harbour.

I was determined, if possible, to make another attempt to block Ostend before the period ended. Although the *Vindictive* had been much knocked about in her upper works, examination showed that the damage she had suffered could be repaired sufficiently in a few hours to enable her to cross the Channel. So

I telephoned at once to the Admiralty, to say I proposed to block Ostend with the *Vindictive*, and this was approved.

It was necessary to trim her to the right draught and fill up all available spaces with concrete to prevent salvage. A large party of soldiers helped to fill bags with rubble and concrete and she was actually ready for sea with three possible days still left. However, there was no suitable day after 23rd April.

The next period—a moonless one—started on 9th May. In the meantime I had obtained another old cruiser, the *Sappho*, and an attempt was made that night, under the command of Commodore Lynes. I took out a flotilla of four destroyers to guard his eastern flank from the nine German destroyers, which we knew had arrived at Zeebrugge. Ill-fortune again dogged this venture, the *Sappho* had a boiler accident and broke down, and a sea fog made it difficult for the *Vindictive* to find the entrance of Ostend, in spite of the excellent arrangements which had been made to mark it with flares. When she did eventually get in, the Captain was killed at a critical moment, when he was about to give the order which would have swung her across the channel. The delay was fatal and the *Vindictive* only blocked about a third of the channel. Two M.L.s gallantly rescued the crew, one suffered many casualties and crawled out to seaward in a sinking condition, and was lying stopped about 2 miles from Ostend, some time after the Dunkirk force had withdrawn, when I happened to see her distress signal and picked them up in the *Warwick*. Shortly afterwards the *Warwick* struck a mine, which destroyed 70 feet of her stern, and it was fortunate that the foggy weather screened us from the powerful batteries within range of which we remained for two or three hours of broad daylight. It was also fortunate that the German destroyers did not appear, as I had to keep one destroyer alongside to steer us, while another towed us home, a lengthy proceeding.

By the time I reached Dover late that afternoon, the Admiralty had issued a statement that Ostend had been successfully blocked; I protested warmly, but they would not withdraw it. I then started preparing for a third attempt with the *Sappho* and an old battleship, the *Swiftsure*, which was to be commanded by Commander Andrew Cunningham—the present Commander-in-Chief of the Mediterranean.

However, our intelligence people reported that the Bruges-Ostend canal could not be used by the destroyers and submarines blocked in Bruges, owing to the canals being silted up, so the Admiralty called the expedition off, after all the preparations had been completed.

Meanwhile our anti-submarine measures were taking heavy toll of the enemy. We learnt after the war that as early as February the ocean going submarines working from the Heligoland Bight were ordered to go North about, which added 7 or 8 days to their passage, before they could reach their killing ground; and in July it was optional for the Flanders submarines to attempt the passage of the Straits; consequently they worked mostly in the North Sea. I think that the last submarine to attempt the passage of the Straits was on 29th August, when she avoided the illuminated area and followed a ship through the safe channel close to the coast, but was detected and destroyed in the controlled minefield —a device invented by Professor Bragg—the operator watching a galvanometer agitate on Shakespeare Cliff pressed a button, and out of the explosion bubble emerged a German officer and two men.

When the tide eventually turned on the Western front and the great offensive was launched on 28th September 1918, by the British 2nd Army, the French Corps and the Belgian Army, I hoisted my flag in a monitor, and the guns of the monitors, which were anchored after dark well within range of the coastal batteries guarding Ostend, and the naval siege guns burst into flame at zero hour. The young naval airmen—despite a westerly gale and driving rain which greatly hampered the co-operation they could have given in finer weather—took the air and rendered much assistance.

During the next three weeks, all the ships and aircraft under my flag co-operated with the Belgian Army. Their first thrust carried the Belgian troops 12 miles through the Houthoulst Forest, well beyond their communications, and for the next few days our young naval airmen supplied them with ammunition and pro-visions—probably the first time, in those days of rigid trench warfare, that troops had been supplied from the air.

The enemy on the coast were kept in a constant state of anxiety by seeing large naval forces, towing barges, closing in to the coast at nightfall.

Actually after our attacks on Zeebrugge and Ostend, aerial photographs showed that the planking of every pier and landing stage had been removed along the coast, for fear of possible landings.

After Ostend and Zeebrugge fell, I received a letter from Marshal Foch's chief Staff Officer thanking me for the co-opera-tion of the Navy and its airmen, declaring that not a single unit or man of the German Corps in the coastal area had been identi-fied in action against the armies further afield.

CHAPTER V

COMBINED OPERATIONS IN THIS WAR

'I pray thee, fear not all things alike, nor count up every risk. For if in each matter that comes before us thou wilt look to all possible chances, never wilt thou achieve anything. Far better is it to have a stout heart always, and suffer one's share of evils, than to be ever fearing what may happen, and never incur a mischance....'   HERODOTUS, Book VII

'Something must be left to chance. Our only consideration should be, is the honour and benefit to our country and its Allies worth the risk? If so, in God's name, let us get to work.'   LORD NELSON

I have told you of the amphibious expedition carried out by Wolfe and Saunders, under the inspiration of the elder Pitt, for the capture of Quebec; of the operations to relieve the Legations in Peking by Allied Naval and Military forces in 1900; and of the Dardanelles Campaign in 1915.

Referring to this last ill-fated enterprise, a German General—Hans Kannenfiesser Pasha—who was with the Turkish Army, in his book on the Gallipoli Campaign, paid a great tribute to the fighting qualities of the British troops and their energetic Commanders in the field, but was very scathing about the working of our War Machine. He said: 'Conversations, minutes and reports preceded the decisive meetings, which again continually postponed the vital decision. So valuable time was lost, and at the Front that moment was lost which contained the possibility of success.' He went on to say: 'The leadership of a war cannot be entrusted to a Limited Liability Company.'

In his *World Crisis* the Prime Minister calls attention to the mistakes and errors which were committed in Downing Street and Whitehall in the Gallipoli Campaign. He says: 'The errors and miscarriages which took place on the battlefield cannot be concealed, but they stand on a lower plane than those sovereign and irretrievable misdirections.'

That was before Mr Lloyd George seized the reins of Government and formed a small War Cabinet, which included statesmen of the calibre of Lord Milner and General Smuts.

Mr Lloyd George may have made mistakes, but with a ruthless disregard of all personal considerations, the faint-hearted and irresolute were eliminated and drastic changes were made, which instilled into the War Machine an admirable will to victory.

I have told you how I was given an absolutely free hand to wage war in the Dover Straits and on the Belgian coast in 1918. In the amphibious operations which I carried out, I strove to profit by the lessons of the past and by the experience I had gained in Combined Operations in which I had taken part.

Mr Lloyd George, supported by his small War Cabinet of statesmen, prosecuted the war vigorously until the Armistice, but in the years that followed the politicians who succeeded to power revived the pernicious Committee system, as a means of avoiding or delaying decisions and shifting the responsibility for Naval, Military and Air matters on to the Service Chiefs, who in their turn, with the assistance of numerous Inter-Service Committees, refrained from recommendations which did not fit in with political requirements, or else acquiesced in political decisions which jeopardized the Empire like the London Naval Treaty of 1930.

Inter-Service rivalries were invariably settled politically on a 50-50 basis—regardless of the merits of the case—which satisfied neither side and left dual control in being, over weapons and services, which was bound to break down under war conditions; and once again Britain found herself at war utterly unprepared— this time in all three Services—to meet the storm and compete with the armies, navies and air weapons developed by the aggressor nations.

That we have weathered the storm we owe in great measure to Mr Winston Churchill's indomitable spirit; taking the helm in

Britain's blackest hour, he roused the fighting spirit of our race, which had lain dormant during the years when 'Peace at any price' and 'Safety First' were almost national slogans. It was not surprising that aggressor nations thought we had become a decadent race, and made their plans accordingly to dominate the world and eliminate the British Empire.

Not the least of many misfortunes, which the nation and our war effort suffered—as the result of our failure to carry the Gallipoli Campaign to a victorious issue—was the elimination of Mr Churchill from any connexion whatever in the conduct of the last war from May 1915, when his Naval colleague—Lord Fisher—deserted him, being unwilling to share with him the responsibility for ordering the naval attack on the Dardanelles to be renewed, when the Admiral on the spot offered to do so, if ordered.

This experience cannot but have had a profound influence on Mr Churchill. For years his 'Gallipoli Gamble' was discredited as a fool-hardy adventure and his judgement was distrusted. During the years that followed the Armistice, when his organizing ability and drive would have been invaluable in helping to prepare to meet the storm before it broke, he was in the wilderness, leading a small band in the House of Commons—of which I am proud to have been one—and striving to wake up the country to re-arm before it was too late.

When war broke out in 1939, Inter-Service Committees and Sub-Committees were flourishing. The Committee of the Chiefs of Staff of the three fighting services had become all-powerful. As one in a position to know remarked to me, in one of our blackest hours, when things were going all wrong in Norway: 'The Chiefs of the Staff will lose this war; we politicians bear all the responsibility, but the Chiefs of Staff have all the power.'

In the Debate in the House of Commons on 7–8th May 1940, which resulted in the overthrow of the Chamberlain Government, Mr Churchill defended the action of the Government over Norway, and declared that they acted on the advice of their responsible Service experts, but added: 'Ministers are not sheltered by the fact that they accept their experts' advice; on the other hand they are very unsheltered if they over-ride their advice.'

A year later—7th May 1941—he said: 'Mr Lloyd George spoke of the great importance of my being surrounded by people who would stand up to me and say No, No, No. Why, good gracious, has he no idea how strong the negative principle is, in the Constitution and working of the British War-making Machine? The difficulty is not, I assure him, to have more brakes put on the wheels; the difficulty is to get more impetus and speed behind it.'

On 24th February 1942 the Prime Minister told the House of Commons about the working of the War Machine with its innumerable Committee meetings, and mentioned that in 1941 the Chiefs of Staff Committee—which he declared: 'conduct the war from day to day and in its future outlook'—had 462 meetings, most of them lasting over two hours! But these meetings did not result in any amphibious operations being undertaken—in spite of all my efforts—although we had a splendid force spoiling for action, and a very wide field for vigorous offensive enterprise.

Nevertheless the Prime Minister accepted all responsibility, saying: 'I take Constitutional responsibility for everything that is done, or is not done, and am quite ready to take the blame when things go wrong, as they very often do, and as they are very likely to do in the future.'

To be 'constitutionally' dependent on a Committee of Experts, who, like all Councils of War, can be relied upon to shrink from responsibility—if there is any possible risk of failure—is a dreadful handicap to labour under, when striving to *make war* against ruthless enemies, who are free from the limitations of democratic Government!

At the beginning of the last war we had an all-powerful modern Fleet at its strategic base, safeguarding the communications of the Empire, carrying and supplying our armies overseas, and generally holding the ring, until the hammer blows of the Army made the enemy sue for peace.

In addition to the modern Fleet in the main theatre, we had a very large force of obsolescent ships, with which to carry out amphibious combined operations on a large scale, and long before the end we had a Naval Air Service second to none, with 2500 aeroplanes developed to fulfil naval functions, which remained under naval control until the war ended, despite its absorption by the R.A.F. in April 1918.

When this war broke out and Mr Churchill became First Lord of the Admiralty once again, he found—thanks to the London Naval Treaty of 1930—a fleet utterly inadequate to fulfil the vast responsibilities the Navy was called upon to undertake. The Naval Air Service was non-existent, and all the Navy possessed under its own control was the Fleet Air Arm, in process of transfer from the R.A.F., consisting of about 260 obsolescent aeroplanes. The other naval functions for which aircraft were absolutely essential were the responsibility of the Coastal Command of the R.A.F., which itself was dependent for all offensive action on the Fighter or Bomber Commands, all three being independent of one another, which was not conducive to efficiency or swift action. The result was that the Germans completely dominated the air over the North Sea, and our shipping and fishing fleet suffered cruel losses, and many opportunities were missed of inflicting losses on enemy ships.

We were told submarines were no longer a menace, owing to recent inventions, an opinion which was not shared by me or any submarine officer.

During the first few months of the war, there was of course no question of carrying out Combined Operations against Germany's limited and heavily fortified coast line; but when she occupied Denmark, and with great daring invaded Norway by sea and air transport—despite the presence of a greatly superior British Fleet within striking distance—a wonderful opportunity was open to us, if it had been pursued with equal daring and enterprise.

Evidently Mr Churchill thought so, because on 11th April 1940 he declared in the House of Commons: 'We were greatly advantaged by what had occurred, provided we acted with the necessary vigour to profit from the strategical blunder which our mortal enemy has made.'

No one knowing our belligerent Prime Minister would doubt for a moment that he personally was in favour of vigorous action, and the Navy at sea were eager for immediate action and spoiling to attack the German ships, which had defied our naval superiority and taken great liberties in Norwegian waters, where they were open to attack.

But Inter-Service Committees were in full swing in Whitehall, irresolution reigned, time passed and golden opportunities were missed.

It is true that British and French troops were promptly carried overseas to capture Narvik and Trondhjem, but a Combined Naval and Military Operation which would have insured the capture of Trondhjem and its aerodrome was never carried out. The aerodrome was the key to the whole situation in Norway, since it would have provided the necessary base for our aircraft; moreover, its use was denied to the enemy, as a Norwegian fort overlooking it was held throughout these operations.

The plan of action was for British forces, which were successfully landed at Namsos and Andalnes, north and south of Trondhjem, to advance on it. Naval co-operation was to be given by the Home Fleet forcing an entrance and landing troops inside the Trondhjem Fiord on 25th April, along the shores of which the Namsos force would have to advance.

The naval attack, however, was abandoned, because the two flank attacks had made good progress, and it was considered by the expert Service advisers in Whitehall that it would be much easier to capture Trondhjem by this means, than incur the risk of possible heavy loss by direct naval attack.

It was known, however, that there were two German torpedo craft in the fiord, but 'It would not have been justifiable to undertake to force Trondhjem fiord for the purpose of cleaning up that very small item'—to quote the official explanation.

Nevertheless those two small torpedo craft defeated the attack from Namsos, which could only advance along the shores of the fiord, owing to the nature of the country, and was doomed to failure, as the German ships were left in command of the fiord. They were able to open fire on the flank of the troops advancing from Steinkjer, and transport and land troops behind the British advance guard, which they destroyed or captured.

General Carton de Wiart, commanding the troops, told me that he had not been warned of their presence and had expected to find British ships in the fiord to co-operate with him.

The only defences at the entrance of the fiord were four thirty-year-old 8 in. guns and a couple of torpedo tubes on a raft, all of which could have been destroyed by the fire of a battleship from outside their range. Two or three destroyers and a couple of old cruisers could then have entered the fiord without any risk, dealt with the German torpedo craft and altered the whole situation in our favour, without risking the valuable ships of the Home Fleet at all.

The Admiralty were given the plan I have mentioned, which was based on that successfully used to destroy the outer forts in the Dardanelles, and were warned of the importance of sending ships into Trondhjem Fïord as early as 17th April, and it is interesting to read in an account by an American journalist—Shirer's *Berlin Diary*—the following: '21st April 1940. A friend of mine in the High (German) Command tells me that the whole issue in Norway hangs now on the battle for Trondhjem. If the Allies take it they save Norway, or at least the Northern half of it. What the Germans fear most, I gather, is that the British Navy will get into Trondhjem Fiord and wipe out the garrison in the city, before the Nazi Forces from Oslo can possibly get there. If it does, the German gamble is lost.'

The extreme caution of the Admiralty in the Norway Campaign was excused because of the fear of risking ships, which might be required in case Italy came into the war. But at that time France was still our Ally and had a superior fleet to the Italians in the Mediterranean.

Another American journalist—Virginia Cowles—who was in Rome at the time, wrote in *Looking for Trouble* that the mess made of the Norwegian Campaign had a disastrous effect there, particularly in face of the initial optimism in London.

Trondhjem and other Norwegian harbours are now heavily fortified and provide safe bases for the powerful modern ships and submarines of the German Navy, which lie there, apparently immune from air attack, on the flank of our communications, a constant threat to our convoys in the Atlantic and on the Arctic route to Russia. This threat can only be countered by constantly maintaining a superior British force in Northern waters.

The failure to take a small risk at Trondhjem to win a great prize certainly had far-reaching effects on the course of the war.

During the Belgian Campaign, I was attached to the King of the Belgians as Special Liaison Officer and had unrivalled opportunities of observing the wonderful results achieved by the German modern war machine—a combination of shock troops dropped by parachute, carried in gliders, rubber boats, or armoured vehicles, supported by tanks and dive bombers, working in perfect unison under one command. Our Army possessed none of these things.

A few weeks after the evacuation of Dunkirk and Narvik, the Prime Minister was evidently turning his thoughts to offensive action, and in July 1940 he sent for me and offered me the appointment of Director of Combined Operations. He told me that I would have under my command the Special Service and Parachute troops being raised, and the landing craft to carry them, and command of the Training and Development Centres which were being set up. He told me to prepare to carry out raids and that I would have command of raiding operations up to 5000 men.

From the Prime Minister's minutes, it is evident that he contemplated delivering amphibious strokes, akin to those launched by the elder Pitt during the Seven Years' War, with the object of keeping the French continually on the *qui vive* along the French coast, and also those potential expeditions which, in a later generation, Napoleon feared.

In the Mediterranean there seemed to be no limit to what might be achieved by highly trained troops, marines and seamen with wholehearted co-operation of the R.A.F. What a vista of opportunity opened! I set to work to organize and train such a force with all possible speed.

I flew up to the airfield on which the parachute troops were being trained and found 100 men, but no suitable aircraft to carry them; those allocated by the R.A.F. were a couple of old bombers, which could only carry eight equipped men, to leave which they had to drop through the bomb hole in the fuselage—a trying ordeal. It happened that there were a couple of American Douglas transport planes on the aerodrome, which belonged to the Dutch Government. They were similar to the planes in which I had flown across America six years previously at a speed of 200 miles an hour; they were much superior to anything that we possessed and were capable of carrying twenty equipped men. I tried to obtain them, but they were required for civil transport work and efforts to obtain Douglas or Boeing planes from America were not successful. However, a few months later, a small force of paratroops were dropped in Southern Italy, where they blew up the big aqueduct carrying the main water supply for the South and disorganized it for about ten days. After this the parachute troops were taken over by the Air Ministry and War Office and I had nothing further to do with them.

Out of these small beginnings an Air-borne Force is being slowly developed, and in time I suppose we shall have one properly equipped with large gliders and transport planes, a force of sufficient strength to play an important part in Combined Operations of the future; but neither the War Office nor the Air Ministry appear to have been in the least interested in the possibility of this kind of warfare, although for many years before the war photographs were published in the papers showing both Russian and German air-borne troops dropping in great numbers from the sky, with guns and even tanks attached to parachutes. We have indeed paid heavily for the obsession, which ruled in the Air Ministry for so many years—to the detriment of the development of Naval and Military aviation—that wars could be won by bombing alone; and the War Office's neglect to keep in step with the progress of modern methods of war.

I do not claim for a moment that the Admiralty is free from criticism because Combined Naval and Military Operations must necessarily at the outset be the Admiralty's responsibility, and the failure to allow us to undertake any of the Combined Operations of any moment, which were projected during the first three years of the war, must rest mainly on the Admiralty's shoulders.

The composition, organization and training of the amphibious striking force of 'Commandos', for which I was responsible, was based on the experience I had gained in the past.

Speed in the approach of the assault force was necessary, in order to effect tactical surprise and land as soon as possible after dark, so a number of fast passenger ships were acquired and equipped to carry as many landing craft as possible.

Since the limitations of sea transport to the scene of action must necessarily be a ruling factor, any redundant personnel in the striking force had to be eliminated, by the administrative staff being cut down to the barest minimum, in order that all available space, both in transports and landing craft, could be used for fighting men.

Volunteers of high morale, eager to take part in hazardous enterprises, were selected and intensively trained in guerilla warfare and *above all night fighting*. In order to get their sea-legs and overcome sea-sickness, every opportunity was taken of embarking them in mine-sweepers and Coast Patrol vessels.

Thus the spearhead of an Assault Force was produced and trained in boat work to a high pitch of efficiency and enthusiasm, which, I am convinced, could have achieved all that the Prime Minister hoped for it, if only the War Machine could have been induced to make use of it; but just as in 1915, vital decisions were being

continually postponed and fear of concealed howitzers—which inflicted neither casualties nor damage; fear of mines—which could
be swept; fear of torpedo tubes—which did not exist, combined
to defeat the Dardanelles enterprise; so in this war fear of air
attack—not really a very formidable menace at night, nevertheless
the bogey of Whitehall—defeated every projected amphibious
operation before it could be launched.

PLANNING COMBINED OPERATIONS

I have been particularly asked to say something about planning.
I told you in a previous lecture that when I was Director of Plans
at the Admiralty in 1917 I submitted a plan for the blocking of
Zeebrugge and Ostend. It gave detailed information about those
ports; the ships which might be made available for the operation,
the manner in which they should be loaded with concrete (after
consultation with a Salvage Company); the possible dates on
which the operation could be carried out with regard to tide and
moon for a night or dawn attack. The plan was in fact a Staff
appreciation, which could not fail to be of value to an Admiral
charged with the execution of the project. It stressed the importance of giving him a free hand. Above all it advanced every
possible argument to overcome the objections which had been
raised from time to time during the past two years against delivering any offensive attacks on Zeebrugge and Ostend. The
detailed planning would of course be carried out by the Staff of
the officer to whom the operation was confided—under his direction, when he had decided on his plan.

In doing this I was fulfilling, I think, the proper functions of a
Staff Officer. It was then for the Board of Admiralty or the War
Cabinet to decide whether the operation was to be carried out,
select the Commanding Officer, give him the Staff appreciation,
ask him if he was prepared to carry it out and had confidence in
his ability to do so.

Then, if he accepted the charge, give him all he asked for, and
back him up loyally, as long as he still had confidence in himself

and enjoyed the confidence of his command. In this war the whole process has been reversed.

For example, when I was Director of Combined Operations, I submitted a plan in outline, which I considered feasible with the resources available, and of great strategic value. It was warmly approved by the Chiefs of Staff Committee.

The Prime Minister, who had originally asked me if I had considered the possibility of such an undertaking, was delighted and declared that 'it would electrify the world and alter the whole strategic situation' in a certain area.

A council of war, attended by the three Service Chiefs and Ministers, presided over by the Prime Minister, after listening to the outline of the plan, unanimously approved of the project being undertaken. Tormenting delays ensued, caused mainly by difficulties in getting decisions for the movements of troops and vessels, which would be required, to the place selected for the training to be carried out. During this time Inter-Service Sub-Committees got to work and did everything in their power to prevent the operation from being carried out; all secrecy was lost, it was discussed by Staff Officers and Civil Servants of all three Services. All the possible hazards and difficulties were exaggerated; its strategical value was discredited, and they succeeded in working on the feelings of the Chiefs of Staff to such an extent, that although they had originally approved of the operation, they decided that the odds were 3 to 1 against it and it was finally cancelled; although I, the officer selected by the Prime Minister to command it, who had worked out all the details and had trained my force to a high degree of efficiency, was confident of success, as were all the soldiers and sailors of my command.

The delays and indecisions which followed the original approval of the plan gave the Germans time to take measures, which certainly added to the hazards, but, in the view of those who were eager to carry it out, did not jeopardize success; and the value of the prize most certainly justified some risk being accepted; and that I am sure will be the verdict of history.

It is of course necessary to employ trained Staff Officers to work out details and plans, but Inter-Service Committees and Sub-Committees which have sprung up since the last war and have flourished exceedingly in peace time have, in this war, become almost the Dictators of military policy, instead of the servants, as they should be, of those who really should bear all the responsibility.

In August 1941 practically the whole of our Amphibious Striking Force was standing by to carry out a large-scale operation overseas; it was very important that a dress rehearsal should be undertaken first, and this was done a few days before the expedition was expected to sail.

The Joint Commanders of the expedition—who had been appointed by the Chiefs of Staff Committee—and an Inter-Service Planning Committee, organized a full-scale exercise, and they declined any assistance or advice from the Directorate of Combined Operations or its Training Centre. A number of shocking miscarriages occurred in the direction and conduct of the exercise, which took no account of the realities of modern war; fortunately the operation never took place.

When criticized by the Director of Combined Operations, those responsible for the planning and execution of the exercise declared that the study of opposed landings was still in its early stages, and that there was still a great deal to be learned. It was only by practical experience on a large scale that faults and difficulties would come to light.

The moral of this unfortunate episode is, that it is not sufficient to train and temper an Amphibious Striking Force, unless those who are to command, lacking practical experience, closely study former operations and make use of the experience already gained.

LOFOTEN RAID

The first raid on the Lofoten Islands in March 1941 was the only raid permitted in Home Waters during the 15 months I was D.C.O. except for small reconnaissance raids on the French coast.

It was carried out by ten troops taken from the 3rd and 4th Commandos, and a Norwegian force of 4 officers and 48 men under the Brigadier commanding the Commando Brigade. They were carried in two passenger vessels fitted up as troopships and equipped with landing craft—two capable of landing a 20 ton tank, or 100 armed men, and six capable of carrying 40 armed men. These vessels were escorted by five destroyers, the senior officer of which was in naval command of the expedition. The object was to raid four ports in the Lofoten Islands, to destroy oil installations and plants for obtaining oil from fish, which had been seized by the Germans, and to capture Germans and Norwegian Quislings. All these objectives were successfully carried out and in addition a number of Norwegians were brought away, who were anxious to join the Norwegian forces in England and Scotland.

About 20,000 tons of shipping was destroyed, including two armed trawlers and a 9000 ton vessel, which had been converted into a factory ship for extracting oil from fish and manufacturing fish meal; also a vessel which had just embarked 2000 tons of fish and fish meal for Hamburg, and was about to sail. It was a great pity that these valuable prizes could not have been brought away, but in view of the proximity of superior German naval forces and aircraft, and the distance from British support, it was not considered practicable.

Owing to the complete surprise and unexpected nature of the attack, no opposition was encountered from the Germans, who were all taken prisoner, except from one armed trawler which put up a gallant fight against overwhelming odds.

It was interesting, however, to note that a senior naval officer remarked—with reference to a suggestion that the destroyers should go in, in close support of the landing craft—that the Military Commander 'did not appear to appreciate the limitations of supporting fire from high velocity Naval guns'. An opinion which is certainly not shared by any soldier or sailor, who watched the destroyers off Gallipoli close in and support troops fighting on the sea flank with guns, pom-poms and machine guns at point blank range; or in this war, by those who were plucked out of Dutch and French ports by destroyers which engaged and smashed up enemy tanks, artillery and infantry, which would otherwise have overwhelmed and destroyed or captured our troops.

Had there been any need for close support at Lofoten, I am absolutely certain that it would have been forthcoming from the young naval officers in command of the destroyers; and once again the present generation would have learnt from practical experience, what they should have learnt from the records of Gallipoli and incidentally those of the early days of this war.

COMBINED OPERATIONS IN THE MEDITERRANEAN, 1941–43

Turning to the Mediterranean, a glance at the map shows clearly that vital and vulnerable enemy communications follow the coastline; not only in Italy and her islands, but also along the African coast.

Is it conceivable that the man who was responsible in the last war for the great strategic conception of attacking the Central Powers where they were weakest—by a wide turning movement through the Dardanelles—rather than concentrating on continuing to attack across the barbed wire on the Western front, was blind to the immediate and immense advantage of shortening the route to the Middle East, by capturing strategic positions in the Mediterranean and delivering surprise amphibious attacks on the enemy's communications? I can bear witness that all these considerations were powerfully and insistently urged by Mr Churchill, but though approved in principle by the Chiefs of Staff Committee, the various Committees and Sub-Committees

of the War Machine succeeded in producing so much obstruction, that action was delayed for some months, until the Germans
had forestalled us and introduced hazards, which the Prime
Minister did not feel able to face without the full support of his
Chiefs of Staff, and that was denied to him.

The difficulty of providing the necessary shipping for more
ambitious enterprises, which the Prime Minister was eager to
carry out—and which in my opinion were feasible—was always
stressed by the Admiralty, but how enormously the shipping
situation would have been relieved, if we had only concentrated
on exercising our predominant Sea Power by driving the Italians
completely out of North Africa and capturing some useful island
bases for our aircraft and light forces, as soon as possible after
Italy came into the war, and before the Germans could intervene,
thus making a safe road to the East for our ships.

Until Italy entered the war in July 1940 it was our highway
to India, our Eastern possessions and the great Dominions of
Australia and New Zealand; but when Italy joined in after
France fell—thinking no doubt that all was over, and wanting a
share of the spoil—the whole situation was changed, and a
tremendous burden was thrown on our shipping and Navy,
since all but very strongly escorted convoys had to go round by
the Cape of Good Hope.

However, when Italy invaded Greece on 28th October 1940,
and thus presented us with the opportunity of making use of
Crete, we were once again 'greatly advantaged', if only the
opportunity for waging amphibious warfare in Combined
Operations of all three Services had been seized in the lifetime of
this opportunity. Crete was a wonderful base from which to
strike, and from which a properly equipped Naval Air Service
could have provided invaluable support and air cover for the
Navy, and have relieved the naval Commander-in-Chief of the
necessity of taking his vulnerable aircraft carriers into waters
within reach of enemy shore-based aircraft.

The Admiralty's failure to insist on such an Air Force being provided placed the most cruel handicap on the Navy, who lost many ships off Greece and Crete for want of the air cover they would have had with a well-organized Naval Air Service. It is a tragedy also, that the War Machine neglected even to develop the aerodromes and defences of Crete and lost this invaluable island base to German air attack and air-borne troops, although their sea-borne expedition was destroyed or repulsed by our ships.

A considerable and well-trained Commando Force, with the means to land rapidly and carry out Combined Operations, could have been in the Mediterranean by the end of November 1940, if the War Machine could only have been induced to move more rapidly. After more than two months of unnecessary and exasperating delays, the Force was about to sail, when the unfortunate 'timing' of a convoy to Malta, in January 1941, had disastrous results—in Whitehall. On the assumption that the Italian 'E' boats at night were a more formidable menace than the Italian aircraft by day, a convoy, which included the aircraft carrier *Illustrious*, went through the Sicilian Narrows in daylight, instead of during the dark hours, as was usual previously. Unfortunately a small force of German dive bombers had just arrived in Sicily and, in the absence of adequate British fighter cover, they succeeded in inflicting considerable damage to the convoy. This so alarmed our cautious War Machine that the already much delayed Commando enterprise was finally cancelled on the eve of sailing.

Instead a small Commando Force was sent round the Cape and did not actually arrive in the Mediterranean until April 1941 and they lay idle in Egypt for many weeks. It is true, however, that their splendidly equipped vessels and landing craft proved invaluable, when the German attacks forced us to evacuate the Army and R.A.F. from Greece and Crete.

Surely our policy should have been to concentrate everything on knocking Italy out of the war before Germany was in a position to intervene, while we had the advantage of the Fleet Air Arm having crippled the Italian Fleet by its attack on Taranto, one of her armies deeply involved in Greece, and her African army defeated and the greater part captured by General Wavell's small force.

Can anyone doubt, in the light of General Wavell's successful campaign in Libya, and General Cunningham's brilliant victories in Abyssinia and Eritrea against the Italians in the winter of 1940–41, that Combined Operations and amphibious attacks on Italian communications and island bases, carried out by the flower of our Army in the Commandos, would have been equally successful against an enemy whose people are really more friendly to us than they are to the Germans? They might well have been completely defeated by vigorous combined action by the Army, Navy and Air Force, before the Germans invaded Greece and Italy.

Our Navy and its Air Service inflicted very heavy losses on the Italian Fleet in Taranto and off Matapan, but the damaged ships have always, apparently, been given the opportunity to repair unmolested, while the Royal Air Force have been engaged on other, perhaps less valuable, operations than concentrating on obtaining command of the sea—which always has been, and always will be, the foundation of all British operations, before victory can be achieved. To obtain this the three Fighting Services must co-operate vigorously.

LITANI RIVER ACTION

The one really successful Combined Operation carried out in the Middle East took place during the invasion of Syria at the Litani River, which held up the Australian advance. The French had blown up the bridge and held a very strongly fortified position on the North side.

The 11th Scottish Commando were landed in three separate detachments in a surprise flank and rear attack of the position, about 4 a.m. on 9th June 1941.

The left detachment struck inland and succeeded in capturing a bridge in the rear, cutting off communications; they also captured a battery and a good many prisoners and caused much confusion.

The centre detachment, under the Colonel, captured the bar-racks, but afterwards got into difficulties and had many casualties.

The right detachment was unfortunately landed on the wrong side of the Litani River, which separated them from their ob-jective—the fortified redoubt at the mouth of the river, which they were to have attacked from the rear. However, the young Major in command—a young cavalry officer—was determined to fulfil his mission, and although by this time it was daylight and they were subjected to very heavy fire from machine-guns, mortars and artillery, which caused many casualties, he obtained a rubber boat from the Australians and got across the river with two other officers and eighteen men and captured the redoubt, afterwards turning one of its guns on to another battery, which commanded the river crossing, and knocking it out with direct hits. They held the position until the next day. This enabled the Australians to cross the river without loss and advance later into Syria.

The Commando's losses were over 25 per cent, including the Colonel and five other officers killed, out of those engaged.

At that time the existence of the Commandos was still a secret, but the action was officially described by the Under-Secretary of State for War as follows: 'The Australians were greatly aided in crossing the Litani River by the landing of "British Infantry" North of the river. They were landed from ships of the Royal Navy, and took part in a very gallant action with decisive results, enabling the Australians to proceed.'

Despite the success of this operation, which illustrated the value of the Commando troops and this form of warfare, in an area in which all the enemy's communications were within reach of the sea, the Military High Command in Egypt decided that Com-bined Operations were all too difficult to mount and proceeded to disband the force of Commandos out there. However, the Prime Minister vetoed this and a young Brigadier was sent out to reform them, but by the time he arrived all that were left were a few officers and men of the 11th Commando and they were expended in a gallant effort to destroy the German Commander-in-Chief—General Rommel—and his Headquarters, 250 miles behind the lines, on the eve of the attack of the 8th Army on 18th November 1941, to dislocate the nerve centre of the enemy at a critical moment. This they succeeded in doing in spite of bad weather and great difficulties in their four-day approach from the sea, with only a small proportion of their force, owing to mishaps caused by the bad weather. Unfortunately, General Rommel was away that night, which robbed them of a complete success, which might well have had a decisive effect on the campaign.

Meanwhile, in Home Waters, a large highly trained amphibious striking force of Commandos, Marines and a regular Brigade which had been training with them, equipped with tanks, artillery and anti-aircraft guns with their special landing craft and fast ships to carry them, was left lying idle at home. It is tormenting to think of what such a force could have achieved under a fighting General like Montgomery, whose appointment to command it was actually suggested.

The Prime Minister declared, when the Libyan Campaign opened in November 1941, that we were meeting the enemy on equal terms in armour, with superiority in the air and with command of the sea. Surely it was the moment to make doubly certain of success, by using our trained amphibious striking force in bold strokes on a large scale against the enemy's communications, which, with air superiority and command of the sea, offered no great hazards but immense possibilities, and might have saved us the humiliations we suffered by the loss of Tobruk and the retreat into Egypt.

It is humiliating too, to us sailors, that it should have been left to the Russians, Germans and Japanese to show us the way to wage amphibious warfare, a form of warfare in which I am positive we could excel, if only our High Command could be induced to face some risks to win great prizes.

On 11th February 1943 the Prime Minister told the House of Commons that the British-American expedition to North Africa 'which has altered the strategic axis of the war...was thought by many experts to be most hazardous before it was undertaken'. He went on to say: 'Very nearly did General Anderson, under General Eisenhower's orders, clear the whole province at a run. *Very little more and we might have achieved everything.* It was absolutely right to try but it failed. The Germans effected their entry, and made good their bridge-heads.'

He also said: 'Very serious battles will have to be fought. Including Rommel's army, there must be nearly a quarter of a million of the enemy in the Tunisian tip, and we must not in any way under-rate the hazards we have to dare or the burdens we have to carry.'

The landing of the British-American expedition in North Africa certainly was a masterpiece of good organization, but the French resistance to be anticipated, against such a powerful and well-equipped force, was not really likely to be very formidable, and trifling to that which the Germans could be relied upon to produce, given 'TIME'. 'The advantage of *time* and *place* in all martial actions is half a victory, which being lost is irrecoverable'; as Drake said in 1587.

Surely it was of *paramount importance* and *worth any risk* to seize the ports of Bizerta and Tunis (where the French resisted the Germans), at the same time as Algiers, by a Combined Operation, and secure the vitally important neighbouring aerodromes before we could be forestalled there—as we were—by German air-borne troops.

The hazards would have been trifling to those successfully faced by the Germans in their bold and enterprising amphibious and air-borne invasions of Norway, Crete and Tunisia.

It is true that a small force of British parachute troops were dropped on Tunisian aerodromes, but as they were completely beyond the reach of any support from the troops landed in Algeria—hundreds of miles away with a difficult range of mountains to cross—the paratroops were overwhelmed when the Germans arrived in force, *without any waste of time*, despite the complete surprise we had succeeded in springing on them but which we had unhappily failed to fully exploit.

The Navy has faced tremendous risks and suffered cruel losses in a succession of military evacuations, in order to save the Army from destruction or capture; but once again the Admiralty shrank from the responsibility of running comparatively light risks to help the Army to the best advantage in their offensive operations.

We possess fast, handy ships with landing-craft, which have been working with the Commandos for more than 2½ years; these could have carried a considerable force of Commandos and Marines with some tanks for a surprise night landing in Tunisia, but these amphibious troops are *still* eating their hearts out at home. Success, which I am confident was within our grasp, would have hastened victory and spared our armies the burden of a long-drawn-out and costly campaign, and would have freed them for offensive action elsewhere.

Fear of air attack was no doubt the excuse for failing to land near Bizerta and Tunis, but if the landing had taken place as early in the night as possible, consistent with tactical surprise, the transports and their escorts could have been well away and under fighter cover before dawn. With the ports and aerodromes in our hands, air support would have been available for further operations, and it should then have been possible to prevent the Germans landing in Tunisia to support Rommel.

RAIDS IN HOME WATERS IN 1942

During the past year (1942) a few small raids have been successfully carried out on the French and Norwegian coasts, under the direction of the Chief of Combined Operations. Two on a slightly larger scale—Vaagso and St Nazaire—were brilliantly successful, and that of St Nazaire particularly achieved valuable results, in destroying the lock gates of the only dock on the French Atlantic coast capable of berthing the *Tirpitz*. Here—as at Zeebrugge in 1918—owing to weather conditions, the R.A.F. unfortunately were not able to co-operate.

The large-scale operation which was carried out against Dieppe was presumably planned by an Inter-Service Planning Committee to meet War Office requirements. We were told that it was a necessary preliminary to the invasion of the Continent, for which the United Nations are preparing.

The object of the raid appears to have been to test the arrangements for landing a considerable force of infantry and tanks on a strongly defended beach and re-embarking it again a few hours later, under cover of a strong force of Fighters—rather an expensive form of experiment.

German batteries on either flank of the town, mounting coast defence guns and howitzers, were sited to cover the approaches to Dieppe and to make it impossible for ships to remain off the port in daylight. It was essential therefore to destroy these batteries, in order to allow the ships to support the attack and cover the withdrawal. This service was confided to two Commandos, under the direction of the Chief of Combined Operations.

The 3rd Commando was to attack the battery near the village of Berneval, about 3½ miles north-east of Dieppe, while the 4th Commando attacked the one behind Varengeville-sur-Mer, 4½ miles west of Dieppe.

The 3rd Commando was standing in towards the beaches in their assault craft, led by a motor gunboat, when they came across a German tanker, escorted by armed trawlers; in the action which took place, the motor gunboat suffered severely and the assault craft were scattered. They were to land at two beaches, one near Berneval and the other near Belleville. A number of craft reached the beach near Berneval, but owing to the naval action were delayed 25 minutes and arrived in broad daylight; they were evidently expected and heavily engaged, suffered severe casualties and were unable to make any progress.

Only one of the boats of the other party reached Belleville Beach. She actually arrived before zero hour and her small party —about 20—landed unopposed. They at once advanced to attack the battery, hoping to meet the men from the other beach. They climbed a well-wired gully and reached the top of the cliff. After waiting a short time for others to join them, their Commanding Officer, realizing that the other party was held up, and not having sufficient force to assault the battery—whose garrison outnumbered them by 10 to 1—took up positions in the rear of it and harassed the guns' crews to such an extent that their fire was only intermittent and quite ineffective. The Commando men only withdrew when their ammunition was nearly exhausted and eventually reached their landing craft, which had remained off the beach for three hours under fire.

The 4th Commando landed at two beaches in the dark without opposition, one near the small village of Vasterival, the other some 600 yards farther west. The first party blew up the wire in a steep gully, climbed up it and engaged the battery with mortars from a wood near by. A few snipers, well camouflaged with foliage, crept forward to within 150 yards of the battery and from well-concealed positions picked off the gunners one by one. In the course of this action a lucky mortar shell blew up a ready ammunition dump near one of the guns, which caused a large fire.

Meanwhile the remainder of the 4th Commando moved inland along the bank of the river Saône and, circling round, entered a wood behind the battery. Here preparations were made to assault. At zero hour to a moment, Spitfires came roaring overhead and swooping down delivered an attack on the battery with their cannon fire. As soon as they had withdrawn, the Commando charged with the bayonet. The two leading officers were killed, but the attack was pressed home and the garrison were all killed, except four who were brought back as prisoners. All the guns were destroyed.

The two parts of the Commando then joined up and made for the beach at Vasterival, where their boats were waiting for them, and by 8 a.m. they were on their way back to England, having carried out a brilliantly successful and well-timed Combined Operation, in which the Navy landed the Army at exactly the right spot at the exact moment and brought them safely back again, and the R.A.F. provided cannon fire just before the zero hour of the assault. The 4th Commando losses amounted to 11 killed. A few Rangers—the United States troops trained since her entry into the war on Commando lines—accompanied the raid and rendered a good account of themselves.

I suppose the plan to land these two Commandos so near dawn was necessary in order not to give warning to the enemy, before the main attack was launched at Dieppe—as ordered by the General Officer responsible for the conduct of the operation—but I think it was running great risks, since it did not allow for any unforeseen delays, with disastrous results, not only to the 3rd Commando, but also to the major operation. At least that is my opinion, based on Gallipoli experience. As events proved, the main landing at Dieppe, against a heavily defended position, did not take place early enough to secure the beach and permit the tanks, which were timed to land after daylight, to make good their landing. They were all knocked out by well-sited anti-tank guns, which could not be dealt with either from the air or the sea. In fact it was 'V' Beach at Helles over again, only this time without the support of the 12 in. and 15 in. high-explosive shell fire, which was much heavier, more formidable and accurate than the R.A.F. attack, which was presumably expected to destroy the beach defences. Apparently the R.A.F. laid some good smoke-screens, but their effect was of course intermittent and could not prevent the destruction of the tanks and the pinning down of the reinforcements, who attempted to land after daylight on a beach which was still strongly held by the enemy, rather than on one where a successful night landing had already made good.

The fighters of the R.A.F., within easy reach of their bases, had wonderful opportunities of destroying enemy planes and of giving good cover to our ships, of which they took full advantage with the greatest gallantry and effect.

The passage of over 300 vessels across the Channel, through a minefield which had to be swept, and their arrival, with only one exception—that of the 3rd Commando—at their destinations at the time selected by the Naval and Military Commanders, was greatly to the credit of the Navy.

The fact that a German tanker, lightly escorted, was passing at the time, was a proof that the Germans had no suspicion an attack on Dieppe was imminent. But it has never been explained why this convoy was not reported to the Naval officer in command in time to be intercepted and dealt with, before it scattered the landing craft and could report the presence of a large force of troops approaching the coast—as it evidently did, with disastrous results.

There were many acts of individual gallantry, and the brilliant success achieved by the 4th Commando, and the heavy toll taken of German aircraft by our fighters, was all to the good, but the loss of over 3000 Canadians with all their tanks was a heavy price to pay for the experience which, we are told, was gained in this ill-conceived and ill-fated enterprise.

This generation was taught afresh at Dieppe the lessons which were indelibly impressed on the memories of all who witnessed at Gallipoli, on 25th April 1915, the heroic but unsuccessful and costly efforts to capture in *daylight* a much less heavily defended beach than that of Dieppe.

Amphibious power is a wonderful possession, but it is very hard to get its value recognized and made full use of, and Combined Operations, with the conflicting interests and responsibilities of the respective Services, are infinitely difficult to organize and execute successfully under our Committee system.

However, many of the handicaps under which we laboured so long have now been removed. After three years of war, the vital importance of unified command has at long last been recognized —although dual responsibility for air weapons still remains to an extent which hampers efficiency.

In North Africa the R.A.F., working so brilliantly with the 8th Army, is no more independent of the Military Commander-in-Chief than his tanks, guns or infantry, but it took three years of reverses and frustration to bring about this admirable co-operation.

The Coastal Command of the R.A.F.—mainly equipped with aircraft which had been developed by the Army and Navy Air Services of the United States—is now at last under Naval operational control, in Home Waters and the Atlantic at any rate; but it was not until we had been at war for 17 months that this vitally essential condition was brought about.

The Directorate of Combined Operations, reduced to an Advisory Committee in October 1941, was re-formed in March 1942 under the charge of a vigorous young Naval officer with a gift for organization and tremendous drive, as 'Chief of Combined Operations', with the acting ranks of Vice-Admiral, Lieut.-General and Air Marshal; it is now recognized as an important part of the War Machine, and a large Combined Operations Command has been established.

With landing craft of all sorts and the ships to carry them, highly trained crews and beach parties, Commandos and Marines, we possess the means to deliver a Combined Operation, which in co-operation with the Air Force and air-borne troops, could form bridge-heads for the invasion of the Continent by our Army, which has been receiving battle training of a nature similar to that which the Commandos have been given since July 1940.

Thus with the Fighting Services working in close co-operation with those of the American and other Allied Forces, we have the means to launch attacks, on a scale which should eventually drive Germany and Japan out of the countries they have seized and bring about final victory—which will ultimately be achieved by Thomas Atkins and his Allied comrades, armed with rifle, bayonet and grenade, and the young officers who lead them so bravely.

Some day soon, let us hope, the brakes on the War Machine will be taken off and the control lever slipped into top gear. But meanwhile time passes, and procrastination, the thief of time, has stolen many golden hours and cost the country dear in life and treasure.

NOTE 1. The infinite value of night fighting was one of the earliest lessons learnt in the Gallipoli Campaign, but training for night fighting was much neglected in the intervening years, until revived in Commando training in 1940.

It is interesting to note that recently General Montgomery's brilliantly successful assaults during his North African Campaign have all been delivered in the dark hours.

NOTE 2. Since this lecture was given (10th March 1943), General Eisenhower, the Commander-in-Chief of all the Allied Forces in North Africa, gave an interview to Allied Newspaper Correspondents on 17th April 1943, in which he is reported to have said: 'We will meet three great obstacles in our final drive for Tunis—land mines, flak and the quality of German troops. The enemy will have a lot of all three and any advances we make now are going to be slow, laborious and costly.'

When asked: 'Why did not the Allies land from the sea in Bizerta and Tunis at the start of the North African Campaign last November?' he replied: 'The chief reason was because the British had learned that enemy aircraft made that section of the Mediterranean almost unbearable to shipping. We simply had to have airfields before we could go so far East.'

In another report it is stated that General Eisenhower, explaining why they did not land at the same time at Bone and Bizerta, said: 'Previous British naval experience in the Western Mediterranean had shown that the danger line was at a point just East of Algiers. Available Carriers (aircraft) were being used elsewhere and probably the cost of going further along the coast in the first dash went *beyond the level of calculated risk.*'

NOTE 3 (20th August 1943). It is very satisfactory to note that in the Sicilian Campaign the Americans made use of amphibious power with great success. Three times when their advance along the North Coast was held up, they landed troops at night behind the enemy's lines to strike at his communications and attack him from the rear.

On 9th August a landing was made at 3 a.m., five miles East of Sant Agata, which took the Germans completely by surprise, a column of reinforcements moving up was scattered and 300

Germans taken prisoners. Thanks to the disorganisation caused in the enemy rear, the main American forces were then able to advance and capture the towns of Sant Agata, as well as San Fratello further inland, which was thus made untenable, and 1500 prisoners were captured.

Three days later (12th August) the Americans landed East of Cape Orlando at the mouth of the Naso River; in spite of opposition, this highly trained and determined task force of American Commandos captured Orlando and the central road to Randazzo, which had decisive results on the whole campaign, since it outflanked this strong enemy key position in the centre, which had held up the Allied Armies for some time, and it fell the following day.

On 16th August the Americans made another landing at Milazzo, which they captured. At the same time a small Commando force from the British 8th Army landed successfully 8 miles to the South of Messina, cutting off the enemy rear guard, which was holding up the 8th Army's advance by mining and demolitions. Messina fell the following morning and the Sicilian Campaign was over.

These very successful surprise night landings behind the enemy lines provide additional evidence of the great value of this much neglected form of warfare, and show what might have been achieved by bold amphibious strokes earlier in the Sicilian Campaign and in the Mediterranean, ever since December 1940, when we first had the means and a specially trained volunteer force of Commandos ready and eager to carry them out.

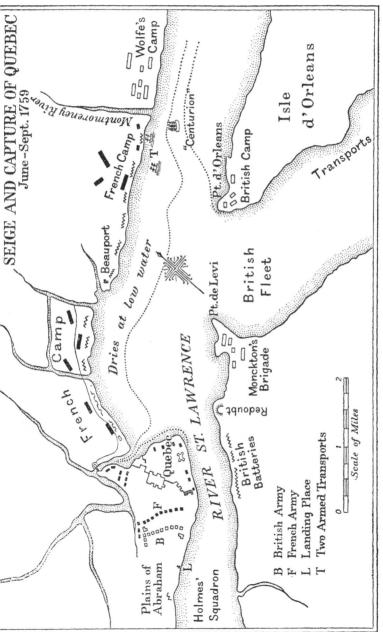

SEIGE AND CAPTURE OF QUEBEC
June–Sept. 1759

Wolfe's Camp

French Camp

Montmorency River

"Centurion"

Beauport

Isle d'Orleans

Pt. d'Orleans

British Camp

Transports

French Camp

Dries at low water

RIVER ST. LAWRENCE

British Fleet

Pt. de Levi

Monckton's Brigade

Redoubt

Quebec

British Batteries

Plains of Abraham

Holmes' Squadron

B British Army
F French Army
L Landing Place
T Two Armed Transports

0   1   2
Scale of Miles

Map I

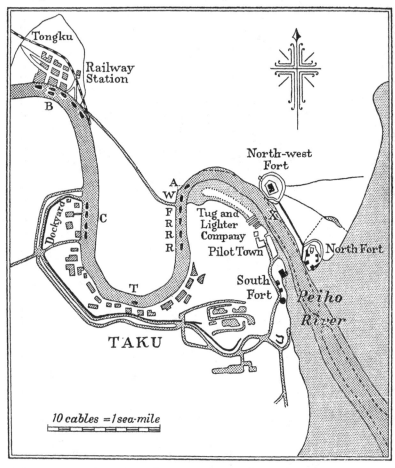

Map. II. Attack on the Taku Forts. Position at midnight, June 16, 1900.

B, American, French, German and Japanese gunboats and two Russian torpedo-boats. C, Four Chinese destroyers. T, tug. R, Russian gun-boats. F, *Fame.* W, *Whiting.* A, *Algerine.* X, Usual berth of *Fame* and *Algerine.*

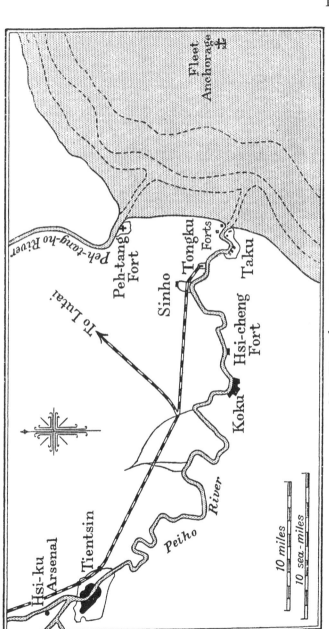

Map III. Taku to Tientsin.

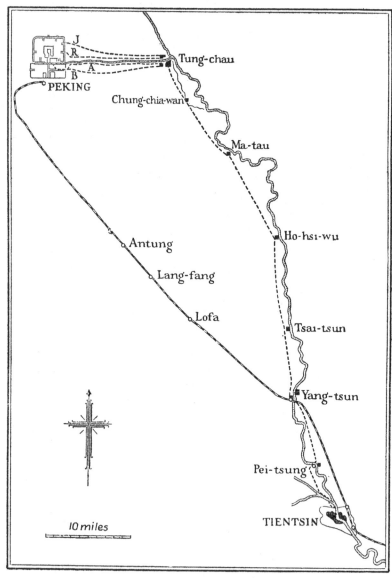

Map IV. Tientsin to Peking.

------ Line of advance. J, Japanese; R, Russians; A, Americans; B, British.

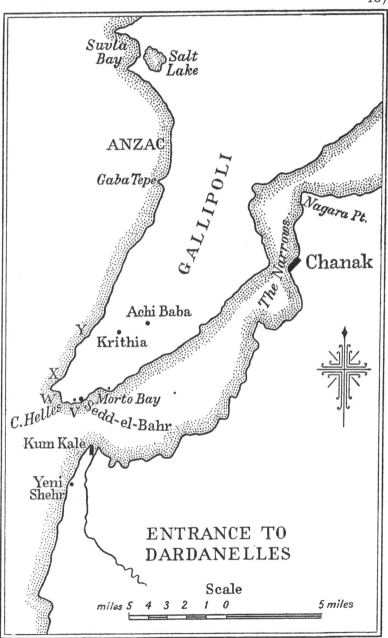

Suvla Bay

Salt Lake

ANZAC

Gaba Tepe

GALLIPOLI

Nagara Pt.

The Narrows

Chanak

Achi Baba

Y

Krithia

X

W

Morto Bay

C. Helles

V

Sedd-el-Bahr

Kum Kale

Yeni Shehr

ENTRANCE TO
DARDANELLES

Scale

miles 5   4   3   2   1   0   5 miles

Map V

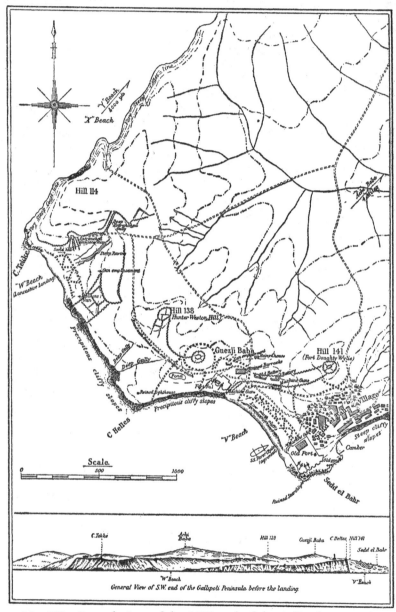

Map VI. General view of the S.W. end of the Gallipoli Peninsula before the landing.

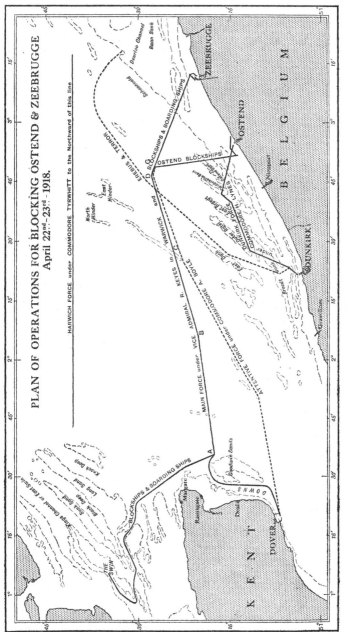

PLAN OF OPERATIONS FOR BLOCKING OSTEND & ZEEBRUGGE
April 22nd.-23rd.-1918.

HARWICH FORCE under COMMODORE TYRWHITT to the Northward of this line

Map VII

109

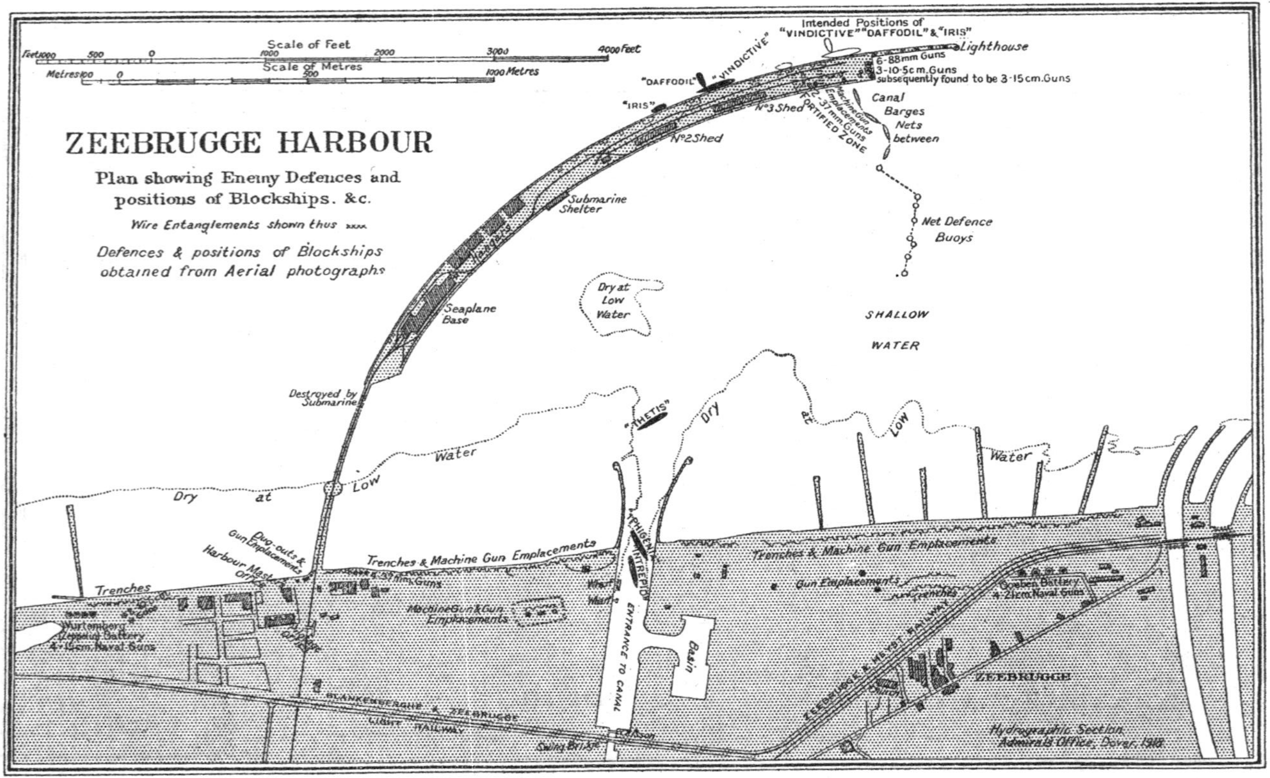
ZEEBRUGGE HARBOUR
Plan showing Enemy Defences and positions of Blockships. &c.
Wire Entanglements shown thus xxx
Defences & positions of Blockships obtained from Aerial photographs
Scale of Feet
Feet 1000 500 0 1000 2000 3000 4000 Feet
Scale of Metres
Metres 100 0 500 1000 Metres
Intended Positions of "VINDICTIVE" "DAFFODIL" & "IRIS"
Lighthouse
6-88mm Guns
3-10·5cm.Guns
subsequently found to be 3·15cm.Guns
"VINDICTIVE"
"DAFFODIL"
"IRIS"
No 3 Shed
No 2 Shed
Machine Gun Emplacements
2-37mm.Guns
FORTIFIED ZONE
Canal
Barges
Nets
between
Net Defence
Buoys
Submarine
Shelter
Seaplane
Base
Dry at
Low
Water
SHALLOW
WATER
Destroyed by
Submarine
"THETIS"
Dry
at
Low
Water
Trenches & Machine Gun Emplacements
Dug-outs & Gun Emplacements
Harbour Mast Office
Trenches
Machine Gun & Gun Emplacements
"IPHIGENIA"
"INTREPID"
ENTRANCE TO CANAL
Basin
Gun Emplacements
Trenches
Goeben Battery
4·21cm Naval Guns
ZEEBRUGGE & HEYST RAILWAY
ZEEBRUGGE
BLANKENBERGHE & ZEEBRUGGE LIGHT RAILWAY
Swing Bridge
Hydrographic Section
Admiralty Office, Dover. 1918

Map VIII

Printed in the United States
By Bookmasters